TELL IT
FROM THE
TORAH

B'raishit ◆ Shemot

Volume I

Written and Compiled by Gedalia Peterseil
Project Editor: Rabbi Yaacov Peterseil

PITSPOPANY

NEW YORK ◆ JERUSALEM

Published by Pitspopany Press

Text copyright © 1997 Gedalia Peterseil

Printing History
First Printing – September 1997
Second Printing – February 1998
Third Printing – February 2000

All rights reserved. No part of this book may be reproduced or transmitted in any form or by any means, electronic or mechanical, including photocopying, recording, or by any information storage and retrieval system, without permission in writing from the publisher.

Design by Benjie Herskowitz

PITSPOPANY PRESS books may be purchased for educational or special sales by contacting: Marketing Director, Pitspopany Press, 40 East 78th Street, Suite 16D, New York, New York, 10021. Fax: (212) 472-6253.

ISBN: 0-943706-95-5 (Cloth)
ISBN: 0-943706-82-3 (Softcover)

Printed in Hungary

CONTENTS

How To Use This Book   4

Foreword   7

Acknowledgments   8

Note: The Index to Vol. I & II can be found at the end of Vol. II

If, after reading through this book, you come up with an original D'var Torah that you would like to share with us...or, if you would like to share your answers to the "Food For Thought" questions...or, if you want to read some interesting answers to the "Food For Thought" questions — contact Gedalia at the Pitspopany Press e-mail: pop@netvision.net.il

HOW TO USE THIS BOOK

Over a period of one year the entire Five Books of the Torah are read in the synagogue. This book is divided into these weekly Torah readings.

In order to familiarize the reader with the Hebrew words and terms used when discussing the Torah readings, we have inserted Hebrew words in transliteration whenever possible. Instead of using the English phrase "weekly reading," we use the Hebrew word Parsha; and instead of calling our forefathers Abraham, Isaac, and Jacob, we call them by their Hebrew names, Avraham, Yitzhak, and Yaacov.

Of course, there are different ways to transliterate Hebrew. We decided that in most cases, the guttural *het* sound, as in *Hanukkah,* would be written with an *h*, rather than a *ch*.

Each chapter in the book covers one Parsha that is read during the week. However, during leap years, more than one Parsha is read on the same Shabbat.

Every Parsha has multiple sections that include:

This is a summary of the weekly Torah reading. The summary is textual, without interpretation. However, when translating from one language to another, sometimes the translation itself can end up being an interpretation. So I tried to find the most logical and understandable translation of words and phrases. When the Torah passages seemed ambiguous, I followed the interpretation of the great Sage, Rashi.

WISDOM
OF THE
SAGES
In this section you can find some short pearls of wisdom that have been passed down from generation to generation.

One of the main sources used in this section is the Midrash, a sort of storehouse of Rabbinic stories and interpretations that gives the reader greater insight into what is happening in the Parsha.

TABLE TALK
DVAR TORAH

This is the main d'var Torah. Its purpose is to develop a theme from the Parsha that anyone can repeat at the Shabbat table. Of course, you may want to add your own ideas or rework ours to fit your audience.

GEMMATRIA The word gemmatria comes from the Greek *geometria*, which means "calculations and measurements." Gemmatria sometimes gets a bit convoluted, but I've tried to make it as easy to understand as possible.

There are many different types of gemmatria. In the most commonly used form, each word in the Hebrew alphabet is given its own numeric value. By combining the numeric value of the letters in different words or phrases, hidden meanings can be found.

Here is a listing of the numeric value of each Hebrew letter.

Aleph = 1	Zayin = 7	Mem = 40	Koof = 100
Bet = 2	Het = 8	Nun = 50	Resh = 200
Gimmel = 3	Tet = 9	Sameh = 60	Shin = 300
Dalet = 4	Yud = 10	Ayin = 70	Taf = 400
He' = 5	Kaf = 20	Pe' = 80	
Vav = 6	Lamed = 30	Tzade' = 90	

FOOD FOR THOUGHT It is important to keep an open mind and question everything we read in order to get a better understanding of it. In this section I suggest a few of the more basic questions found in the Parsha which you may want to think about. Take this opportunity to think of questions yourself.

TELL IT WITH A SMILE The Talmud Shabbat (30b) tells us that the great Sage, Rabbah, would start his lectures with a joke. Rabbah realized that humor is an important vessel with which to clear the mind, enabling one to concentrate and understand better.

We tried to find humor that would relate to the Parsha. See if you can find the connection.

THE HAFTARAH CONNECTION

The source for reading the Haftarah comes from the Talmud Megilah (21a) which says that after reading the weekly portion, we must read a portion from the Prophets which is somehow connected to the Parsha.

There are a number of reasons given for this:

1) The commentator, Livush, says that King Antiohus of Greece prohibited the reading of the Torah in public. The Sages decreed that instead of reading from the Torah, the people should read from the Prophets. Every Parsha was given a Haftarah that would remind listeners what the Parsha was about. Even after the decree was abolished, the custom of reading the Haftarah continued.

The word Haftarah, according to some sources, comes from the Hebrew word *patur*, which means "exempt." Since there was a time when the Haftarah was read instead of the Parsha, the Haftarah was considered to exempt the listener from the Torah reading.

2) In ancient times it was the custom for everyone to stay in synagogue and study the Prophets after daily prayers. Later on, this custom disappeared because people had to hurry off to work. In modern times, the custom was reinstated on Shabbat, when one is prohibited from working.

This helps us understand another definition of the word Haftarah — "after." The Haftarah comes *after* the Torah reading. It signifies the end of the morning prayers.

FOREWORD

This book was written after my son, Gedalia, came back from working with the Jewish community in Cape Town, South Africa. He was chosen to be part of a group sent there from Israel to develop Torah outreach programs.

Gedalia's experiences in Cape Town had a profound effect on him. He gained important insights into the needs of Jewish communities in the Diaspora. But he did not want what he had learned to be simply an intellectual exercise; he wanted to *do* something, to develop something that would make Torah learning accessible to as many people as possible.

This book brings basic Jewish knowledge to young adults and their parents. It helps the reader to better understand the Parsha (weekly Torah reading) and some of the deeper layers of Torah thought.

Rabbi Yaacov Peterseil

This book has been bubbling inside me for quite a while. After working in the *heimishe* Cape Town community, I saw that there was a need for a book on the Parsha that would reach both teens and adults. So many people in Capetown had a sincere thirst and desire to learn; unfortunately, many lacked the basic tools to fulfill their desire.

Another reason for writing a book like this stems from my personal Shabbat experiences. In my parents' home, Shabbat is the time when the family gets together and bonds. There is nothing that moves me more than our Shabbat meals together. An integral part of this wonderful experience is the *d'var Torah* — words of Torah — spoken at the meal.

When I was younger, it wasn't always easy to find something cogent to say at the table. Sometimes, after I finished my d'var Torah, the silence of those at the table was less a sign of awe than bewilderment. I could have used a book like this then. That's why I have made a special effort to include with each Parsha a *Table Talk* section that has a d'var Torah on a mature level, yet is easy to comprehend.

I hope you *enjoy* reading this book. I emphasize the word enjoy. The Torah is a way of life, and just as in life you sweat and toil to get things done, so too, the Torah demands a great deal of mental exertion. But just as in life there are many moments of joy as well, so too, when you study Torah, it is a source of joy and happiness for all those who partake in it.

Gedalia Peterseil

Acknowledgments

I would like to begin by thanking God for teaching me the important lesson of strength and perseverance, and for giving me the ability to finish this book.

A special thanks goes to my parents, Yaacov and Tamar, my siblings, Tehila, Shlomo, Nachum, Tiferet, Temima, Yosef, Todahya, and Tanya, and my brother-in-law Nitay, for giving me the time and support needed to complete the task.

I could not have written the book on my own, and therefore would like to thank Nadav Kidron, Reuven Gafni, Zeev Jacobson, and Ofir Saadon for coming up with some of the beautiful divrei Torah that appear in the book. I would also like to thank Shlomo Peterseil for taking the time to gather many of the gemmatria. I am also very grateful to Rabbi Macy Gordon, a wonderful Rabbi, and friend, whose cogent comments were invaluable.

Let me not forget the Production Director at Pitspopany Press, Chaim Mazo, who managed to get this book printed on time, and Wendy Bernstein, a first-class editor and proofreader.

In *Ethics of the Fathers* 6:5, we learn that "Anyone who repeats something in the name of the person who originally said it, brings redemption to the world." To give credit where credit is due is very important. For that reason, we have listed the commentaries from whom we have taken certain material at the end of the book.

The humorous anecdotes in the book have been compiled over a long period of time. But I would like to make special mention of Henry Spalding's *Encyclopedia of Jewish Humor* (Jonathan David Publishers) — which, for me, is the bible of Jewish humor.

THE BOOK OF
B'RAISHIT

בראשית

God Creates the World in Six Days and Rests on the Seventh

On day one, *God creates heaven and earth, which are filled with darkness and disorder. Then God says, "Let there be light!" He separates between the darkness and light, and night and day are created.*

On the second day, *God creates the heavens above, which He separates from the waters below.*

On the third day, *God brings all the waters of the world together, creating the continents and the oceans. God also creates the grass and the fruit-bearing trees on this day.*

On the fourth day, *God creates the sun, moon, and stars to distinguish between night and day, and for counting the days, months, and years.*

On the fifth day, *God creates the fish in the water, the birds in the sky, and all the crawling insects. He blesss these animals, saying, "Be fruitful and multiply."*

On the sixth day, *God creates the beasts and animals that live on land. God then says, "We will make man in our image!" And God creates Adam*

God completes everything and rests on the seventh day.

He calls this day Shabbat, which in Hebrew means "rest," sanctifies it and makes it holy.

Hava Is Created

After God creates Adam, He tells him to give names to all the different animals. But as he does this, Adam realizes that he is the only one without a mate. God puts Adam to sleep and from one of his ribs creates woman. Adam names her Hava (Eve), which means "life" in Hebrew, for she will become mother of all mankind.

God wants Adam and Hava and their descendants to rule the world. He blesses them, saying, "Be fruitful and multiply."

The Garden of Eden

God plants a garden, the Garden of Eden, and there he puts Adam and Hava.

God tells Adam that he may eat from any tree in the Garden, except the Tree of Knowledge. If he eats from this tree, he will die.

The snake is the slyest of all the creatures living in the Garden. The snake convinces Hava to eat from the Tree of Knowledge by telling her, "God knows that when you eat of the tree you will be like God, knowing what is good and what is evil." Hava is convinced and takes a bite of the tree's fruit; then she persuades Adam to eat some of the fruit.

After eating the fruit, Adam and Hava suddenly realize that they are naked and make clothes from fig leaves.

Then they hear the Voice of God in the Garden. They are scared and try to hide.

When God asks Adam why he is hiding, Adam says he was embarrassed because he was naked. God confronts Adam, asking, "Who told you that you were naked? Did you eat of the

Tree of Knowledge?" Adam admits that he has, but blames Hava for giving him the fruit. Hava says the snake convinced her to eat the fruit.

Punishments

God metes out punishment to all three sinners.

The snake will forever have to crawl on its belly and eat the dirt of the earth. And there will always be hostility between the snake's descendants and Hava's.

Hava and her descendants will find childbearing painful. Also, their husbands will rule over them.

Adam and his descendants will have to work for their food. The soil will only produce if man works it.

Adam and Hava are expelled from the Garden of Eden.

Murder One: Kayin Kills Hevel

Adam and Hava have two children. The firstborn, Kayin, is a farmer; the second, Hevel, is a shepherd.

One day the brothers are in a field and Kayin decides to bring an offering to God from his produce. Hevel, too, brings an offering, from his flock. God accepts Hevel's offering, but not Kayin's. In a fit of anger Kayin kills his brother.

God asks Kayin, "Where is your brother?" Kayin replies, "Am I my brother's keeper?"

As punishment for his terrible deed, God decrees that Kayin will have to wander across the world for the rest of his life. However, God forbids anyone to kill Kayin.

Ten Generations

Later, Adam and Hava have another son, Shet. From Shet and his descendants, the world becomes populated.

Altogether, there are ten generations between Adam and Noah. Two of the more notable descendants of Adam are:

Hanoch: He walked with God.

Metushelah: The oldest man in history, he died at 969 years old.

As time passes, the people of the world grow exceedingly immoral. Only Noah finds favor in the eyes of God.

WISDOM OF THE SAGES

"It was evening, it was morning..." (1:5)

Shouldn't the order be reversed? Doesn't morning come before night?

In the Parsha we learn that, in the order of creation, night came before day. That's why Shabbat and all of the Jewish holidays begin at night, and not in the morning.

The Midrash tells us that at creation, the sun and moon were of equal size. But the moon complained to God, saying: How can there be two rulers in the sky? For the moon's unwillingness to share power, God punished it by reducing its size and diminishing its brightness. From the light that God took from the moon, He created the stars. That's why we see the stars shine at night, and not during the day!

"And from the fruit of the tree...you shall not eat from it, nor shall you touch it." (3:3)

The above verse tells us what Hava said to the snake. It is what God told her, except she added the last phrase, the prohibition of touching the tree. Rashi points out that by adding to God's commandment, Hava brought about her own downfall. After hearing her version of what God said, the sly snake pushed Hava into the forbidden tree, proving to her that nothing would happen if she touched it. After that, it was easy for the snake to convince her that nothing would happen if she ate from it as well.

1. Why does the Torah begin with the creation of the world? Why not begin with the first mitzvah, or the Exodus?

2. After Adam and Hava sinned by eating the fruit of the Tree of Knowledge, the Torah says that they realized they were naked. What is the connection between these two concepts?

3. After Adam and Hava made their clothes, God asked Adam, "Where are you?" Didn't God, who is All Knowing, know where Adam was? What was He trying to do by asking this question?

Et Ha'or (1:4)

By studying Torah and keeping all of the commandments that God gave us, we will see the Light?

In Hebrew, "the light" is *et ha'or*. Its numeric value is 613, which equals the number of commandments in the Torah. Add each letter of *et ha'or* and it equals 613!

15

TABLE TALK
DVAR TORAH

God punished the snake for convincing Hava to eat from the fruit of the Tree of Knowledge. From now on the snake would have to crawl on its stomach and eat dust.

The first part of the snake's punishment, that it would crawl on its stomach, seems to make a lot of sense. It is definitely a punishment to have to crawl on your stomach all day. To see the world from a height of about three inches can't be much fun.

However, the second part of the punishment – eating dust – doesn't seem to be a punishment at all. It isn't a punishment to make an animal eat animal food. For, just as fish eat fish food and don't consider it a punishment, snakes eat the insects that crawl in the dust without considering that a punishment. Why should a snake care what it eats, if the food sustains it?

We may even say that the punishment was actually a blessing! Dirt is plentiful. Imagine what it would be like if no matter where people lived, there would always be plenty of food. Starvation would be a thing of the past!

Rabbi Shmuel Grainmen explains this punishment using the following parable:

There was a very wealthy king who had a son. The princes grew up and went on his way. The king kept an eye on him and made sure that the prince always had enough money to buy what he needed. Since the prince had all his needs taken care of, he very rarely found reason to visit his father. The king was not happy about this. One day, he decided to stop sending money to his son. When the prince realized what was happening, he rushed to his father to ask for more funds. The king, glad to see his son, agreed. But from then on the prince never again took his father for granted, and came to visit him daily.

The snake, like the prince at the beginning of the story, has all his needs met. And because he never needs to ask for anything, never needs to connect with God, he never remembers Him. That is the worst punishment of all — not feeling the need to relate to God.

We, on the other hand, like the prince at the end of the story, realize that God controls everything. If we want a good harvest, we have to work, and pray. We do not get our sustenance just because we plant our fields or go to work. We are forced to keep in touch with God, to keep the connection open all the time.

THE HAFTARAH CONNECTION

(Yeshayahu 42:5)

There are two connections between the Parsha and the Haftarah.

First, the Parsha begins with the creation of the world. In the Haftarah, the prophet Yeshayahu reminds the Jewish nation that God, who is the creator of the world, continues creating every day. Creation is not something that was done just once. It is an ongoing miracle.

Second, in the Parsha, man is the only creature given the power to choose between right and wrong. In the Haftarah, Yeshayahu tells the people that God created the Jewish nation in order to be a "light for the nations." It is their responsibility to show the nations what is right, so that they, too, can become closer to God.

 **TELL IT WITH A SMILE**

Reb Pindrop, the town philosopher, came into the Rabbi's study very upset.

"What is it, Reb Pindrop?" asked the Rabbi, concerned.

"I have had a strange and disquieting thought," the philosopher answered.

"Tell me what's troubling you," said the Rabbi.

At first, Reb Pindrop did not answer. It was so quiet in the room that you could hear a pin drop. Finally, Reb Pindrop spoke, "What if all humans became one gigantic man? And what if all the trees of the earth became one gigantic tree? And what if all the axes became one gigantic axe? Now supposed the man took the axe and chopped down the tree and it fell into the ocean..."

"Yes, go on! What then?" asked the Rabbi.

Reb Pindrop leaned over to the Rabbi, took a deep breath, and continued, "Can you imagine what a tremendous splash that would make?"

Q) How do we know that baseball was created on the first day?

A) Just look at the English translation of B'raishit— *"In the Big Inning!"*

נח

THIS WEEK IN THE PARSHA

The Flood

Noah was a righteous man in his generation, who walked in the path of God.

God tells Noah that, since the world is very corrupt, He is going to destroy it by bringing a flood. Only Noah will be saved.

Noah is commanded to build a three-story ark, 300 cubits (one cubit is approximately two feet) in length, 50 cubits in width, and 30 cubits in height.

After Noah builds the ark, God tells him that a torrential rain will begin in seven days and last for 40 days and 40 nights. Noah is to bring his wife, his three sons — Shem, Ham, and Yafet — and their wives into the ark. Noah is also to bring aboard a male and female of all the non-kosher animals and seven pairs of all the kosher ones.

Noah is 600 years old when God floods the world.

Noah Leaves the Ark

The waters rise for 150 days and then begin to subside. The ark rests on the peak of Mount Ararat. Forty days later, Noah sends out a raven to find dry land, but it returns unsuccessful. Seven days later he sends out a dove, which also fails to find land. Noah waits another seven days before sending the dove out again. This time the dove returns with an olive branch in its beak. After seven more days, Noah sends out the dove one last time. It never returns.

God appears to Noah and tells him it is time to leave the ark.

Noah Builds an Altar

Noah leaves the ark and builds an altar to thank God for saving him. He makes sacrifices to God from the kosher animals.

God tells Noah that the fear of man will be instilled in every animal. He also tells him that he may eat meat; however, there is a prohibition against eating a limb taken from a live animal. In Hebrew, this commandment is known as *Aiver Min Hahai.* God further tells Noah that since man was created in God's image, it is forbidden to kill another human. Then God gives Noah the commandment to be fruitful and multiply.

God shows Noah the rainbow, which will serve as a sign for man and a reminder for God of His promise to never again destroy the world with a flood.

Noah Curses Ham's Descendants

Noah plants a vineyard and when his grapes ripen, he makes wine and gets drunk. While he is sleeping, Ham sees his father's nakedness, but Shem and Yafet take a blanket and cover their father without looking at his naked body. When Noah wakes up, he curses Ham's descendants, starting with his son, Canaan. But Noah blesses Yafet and Shem. Among Shem's descendants is Terah, the father of Avram (Avraham).

Noah dies at 950 years of age, 350 years after the Flood.

The Tower of Bavel

After the Flood, the whole world is united and speaks one language. The people want to make a name for themselves, and decide to build a tower that will reach the heavens. They are also afraid that God may scatter them.

God sees that their unity and the fact that they speak one language is being used for an unworthy purpose. He mixes up their language so that they cannot understand each other. They are then dispersed throughout the world. The place where they rebelled against God is called *Bavel*, which in Hebrew means "mixed."

WISDOM
OF THE
SAGES "He was perfect in his generation..." (6:9)

The Talmud explains these words in two opposite ways:

The verse could be understood as lauding Noah by saying that, even though his generation was an evil one, Noah still managed to be righteous. Or, it may be criticizing Noah, saying that only because his generation was so evil did he appear to be so righteous. Had he lived in Avraham's generation, perhaps he wouldn't have been considered so righteous.

"Cursed is Canaan..." (9:25)

After Noah awoke and understood what had happened to him, he cursed Ham's son, Canaan. Why was the son cursed and not the father?

Our Sages tell us that Ham didn't want Noah to have another child because he didn't want to share the world with any other siblings. Since Ham wanted to eliminate all future generations, Ham's descendants were cursed, starting with Canaan.

❖

"And we will make a name for ourselves, so that we won't be scattered across the land." (11:4)

The people built the Tower of Bavel because they wanted to make sure God would not disperse them. They wanted to maintain their universal unity. Wasn't that a noble ideal?

The Kli Yakar says that real unity is only noble when its purpose is to create a better world. When people are united for evil reasons, the unity is neither noble nor real because one person is seeking power, another fame, and yet another fortune. Their goals are never the same, so the unity cannot be real.

1. According to the Parsha (6:13), God destroyed the world because it was full of injustice. The Talmud Sanhedrin (108a) defines injustice as "theft." Is theft a valid reason to destroy an entire world?

2. Noah is given two different titles during two different stages of his life. At first he is called "a righteous man" (6:9). After he leaves the ark, he is referred to as "a man of the earth" (9:20). Why the different descriptions? Has Noah fallen somehow?

3. When we see a rainbow in the sky, our first impulse is to comment on its beauty. When we take into consideration the reason God gave us the rainbow, what, in fact, should our reaction be?

TABLE TALK DVAR TORAH

God chose Noah to survive the Flood because, as He puts it, "I have seen you as a righteous man in this generation."

Some Rabbis take the words "in this generation," literally. Compared with the generation of the Flood, Noah was a righteous man, but had he lived in Avraham's generation he would not have been considered a righteous person.

But why did the Sages find fault with Noah?

Perhaps we can find a clue from a comparison of the two arks mentioned in the Torah.

Both Moshe and Noah were rescued by an ark, but their arks were different. Besides the difference in size, Noah's ark had double insulation — "And you shall smear it from the inside and outside with tar" — while Moshe's ark was insulated only from the outside.

What does this indicate?

Both Noah and Moshe lived among people who needed their help. They were expected to help the sinners of their generation without being influenced by them.

Noah's ark was protected from the elements inside and out, like a cocoon. And that was how Noah insulated himself, inside and out. He wasn't influenced by those around him, nor did he strive to influence others. He didn't seem to care whether the rest of the world went "down the drain."

Moshe, on the other hand, was insulated from the outside, and thus careful not to be influenced by the negative forces around him. But he was able — and willing — to influence others. He reached out to those who needed help.

From all of this, we learn that God expects us to do all we can to protect ourselves from the wicked winds that sometimes batter us, but He expects us go out into the world and help those who need us.

 What sins did Noah's generation commit that would cause God to bring such a devastating flood?

By using gemmatria, we see one example in the phrase, *ki malah ha'aretz hamas mipnayhem,* "for the world is full of evil doings," (6:13). It's numeric value is 735. The words for incest, *giluy arayot,* also adds up to 735.

"But Noah and those who were with him in the ark, survived." (7:23) The numerical value of "But Noah," *Ach Noah* is 79. The use of the extra word "But" indicates, according to the Rabbis, that perhaps Noah and his family were not the only humans who survived. It seems the giant, Og — whose name also has a numerical value of 79 — held onto the ark and survived. He will appear later in the Torah.

TELL IT WITH A

 Two of the brightest scholars in Chelm — if not the whole world — were discussing the difficulties in learning how to spell in Hebrew.

"Let me ask you a question," said one.

"Ask," replied the other.

"Who needs a *gimmel* in the word Noah?"

"But there is no gimmel in Noah."

"Tell me, why shouldn't there be a gimmel in Noah?"

"But who needs a gimmel in Noah?"

"Now just a minute," said the first student. "That's the same question I asked you, 'Who needs a gimmel in Noah?'"

THE HAFTARAH CONNECTION

(Yeshayahu 54:1)

In the Parsha, God floods the world, destroying almost all its inhabitants. The world is left barren and desolate, yet in a sense, God has prepared the world for new, more worthy inhabitants to populate it.

In the Haftarah, the prophet Yeshayahu consoles the land of Israel because the Jews are exiled throughout the world. Yeshayahu says, "for this is as the waters of Noah to me," comparing the Exile to the Flood. The prophet tells the land that the Jews will return with renewed strength, better than they were before. The reason for the Exile was to destroy those who were not worthy to live on the land, and to allow those who would be worthy inhabitants to return.

Avram Leaves his Homeland

God appears to Avram and tells him to leave his homeland and go to a land that He will show him. God assures Avram that his descendants will become a great nation. All those who bless Avram will be blessed; all those who curse him will be cursed. So, at the age of 75, Avram and his wife, Sarai, together with Lot, Avram's nephew, leave Haran and travel to the land of Canaan.

Avram Goes to Egypt

When a terrible famine spreads over Canaan, Avram decides to go down to Egypt. Seeing how beautiful his wife is, and afraid that someone will kill him in order to take her, Avram tells Sarai to pretend she is his sister.

When the Egyptians see how beautiful Sarai is they take her to the Pharaoh. He gives Avram many presents in order to purchase Sarai. God strikes Pharaoh and his household with a plague, which leads Pharaoh to suspect that Avram and Sarai are actually married. Pharaoh is angry with Avram for lying about the relationship. He gives Sarai back to Avram and sends them both away.

Avram and Lot Go their Separate Ways

Avram leaves Egypt a wealthy man and, together with Lot, goes to Beit El. There, the shepherds of Lot and the shepherds of Avram have an argument and Avram and Lot split up. Lot decides to live in Sodom, even though the people there are very wicked.

Following Lot's departure, God appears to Avram. God tells him that all the land that he sees will eventually belong to his children. They will be as numerous as the dust of the earth.

Avram Rescues Lot

A war erupts between four kings, led by King Kidarlaomer, and five other kings who had previously been ruled by him. Kidarlaomer's forces win and, in the ensuing battle, conquer and loot Sodom. Lot is captured.

When Avram hears that his nephew has been captured, he takes 318 of his followers and chases Kidarlaomer and his men. Avram defeats them and recaptures the stolen property and prisoners.

The king of Sodom congratulates Avram and offers to let him keep all the booty; his only request is that the people be returned to Sodom. Avram not only returns all the people, but refuses to take anything for himself. He does insist, however, that those who fought with him receive a share of the spoils.

God Gives Avram a Sign

God appears to Avram and tells him that He is watching over

him. When Avram reminds God that he is childless, God assures him that his children will one day be as numerous as the stars.

Avram asks God for a sign that he will inherit the land. God tells him to take three calves, three goats, three rams, a turtledove, and a young pigeon. Avram cuts all the animals into two, except for the birds. Then, as the sun begins to set and Avram becomes sleepy, he is suddenly overcome by a great dread. God tells Avram that his descendants will be slaves for 400 years, but that they will return to the land with great wealth. When the sun goes down, a pillar of fire passes between the cut pieces of the animals. On that day God makes a special "Covenant Between the Pieces," known in Hebrew as *Brit Bain Habetarim,* with Avram, promising him the land of Canaan.

Sarai and Hagar

Ten years after they return to Canaan from Egypt, Sarai remains childless. Wanting Avram to have a descendant, she gives Avram her servant, Hagar, as a concubine. Hagar becomes pregnant and begins to taunt her mistress, Sarai.

Sarai tells Avram that it is his fault that Hagar mistreats her. Avram tells Sarai to do whatever she pleases with Hagar. Sarai works her so hard that Hagar eventually runs away into the desert. An angel meets Hagar and tells her to return to Sarai. The angel informs her that she will give birth to a son; his name will be Yishmael, which means "God will listen." He will be a wild man, his hand against every man, and every man against him.

When Avram is 86 years old, Hagar gives birth to a son and Avram calls him Yishmael.

Avram's New Name and the Brit Milah

When Avram is 99 years old, God renews his promise to give him many descendants. In return, Avram must continue to walk before God and be pure. God then changes Avram's name to Avraham, which means "the father of many nations."

God gives Avraham the covenant of *brit milah* to show that he and his children are the chosen people. Every male child is to be circumcised on the eighth day after birth. Whoever is not circumcised will be cut off from the nation.

God Changes Sarai's Name

God tells Avraham that He is changing Sarai's name to Sarah, and that she will give birth to a child. Avraham laughs, thinking, "Can a man of 100 and a woman of 90 really have a child?" Perhaps Yishmael should be his chosen heir. But God insists that Sarah will bear him a son, and Avraham will name him Yitzhak. God also tells him that Yishmael will become a great nation.

Avraham Fulfills God's Commandment

Avraham circumcises himself, Yishmael, and all the males of his household. Avraham is 99 years of age and his son 13 years old when they are circumcised.

 When God changes Avram's name to Avraham, He tells Avraham that he will be *av hamon,* "'the father of many." The

29

gemmatria for this phrase is 104. This phrase is used twice during the conversation, so together the numeric value is 208.

The gemmatria of Yitzhak, Avraham's son, is also 208. From this we see a hint that the chosen nation is going to stem from Yitzhak, and not Yishmael.

WISDOM
OF THE
SAGES
The Midrash explains how Avraham came to believe in God:

When Avraham was three years old, he looked up at the sky one night and saw the stars. He was so overcome by this sight that he assumed the stars were God, so he bowed to them. Then, in the morning, the stars disappeared, and the sun rose. Avraham then thought that the sun was more powerful than the stars, so he bowed to it.

At night, the sun sank and up came the moon. So, Avraham decided that if the moon could make the sun disappear, it must be more powerful than the sun, so he bowed to it.

In the morning, when the sun rose again, Avraham realized that the sun, moon, and stars were part of a cycle. Something greater must be controlling them. It was then that he realized that God works "behind the scenes" to make the world function.

"The whole land that you see I will give to you..." (13:15)

God promised Avraham that all the land, as far as his eyes could see, would one day be his. God also told Avraham that his descendants will be as numerous as the dust on the land.

If the prophecy is fulfilled and Avraham's descendants become as numerous as the sand, how will they fit into the land he is looking at?

Just like there is always enough room in a mother's house for all her children — no matter how many children she has — so too, there's always enough room for the Jewish people in Israel!

 **1. Avraham let Lot choose where he would like to live. Avraham said he would go the opposite way. Had Lot picked Hevron, Avraham would have had no choice but to go to the evil place, Sodom. How could Avraham take that chance and let Lot choose?**

2. When Avraham and God made the Brit Bain Habetarim, Avraham cut all the animals in two, except for the birds. Why didn't he cut the birds, too?

3. If brit milah is a covenant for the Jews, why did Avraham circumcise all his slaves as well?

TELL IT WITH A

 The expectant couple met with their friend, the mohel.

"So what do you think?" asked the husband. "Is it a boy or a girl?"

With a wink in his eye, the mohel said, "Boy or girl, it doesn't matter to me just as long as there's a brit!"

A devout young Jew left his village in Russia to seek out his fortune in America. Many years later, after having amassed a fair share of wealth, he decided to return to the old country for a visit. His 80-year-old mother barely recognized him.

"Your clothes are all leather," she complained.

"Well, Mama," he said, "everyone in America dresses like this."

"But what happened to your beard?" she asked.

"Nobody has one in America," he gently replied.

"At least you still keep kosher," she said hopefully.

"To tell you the truth, it is very hard," replied the honest son.

Then suddenly a fearful thought struck her.

"Son," she asked hesitantly, "are you still circumcised?"

THE HAFTARAH CONNECTION

(Yeshayahu 40:27)

In the Parsha, God explains the path of life that Avraham must take. God tells Avraham to leave everything behind and to follow God. Avraham has great confidence in God; that confidence enables him to defeat the neighboring kings in battle.

In the Haftarah, the prophet Yeshayahu consoles the Jewish people, who think God has deserted them. The prophet explains that what makes the Jewish people successful is their confidence in God. As long as the people are confident of their relationship with God, they will overcome all obstacles.

TABLE TALK
DVAR TORAH

G od appears to Avraham and tells him to leave his father's house, his land — everything of any importance to him — and make his way to an unknown place. God was, of course, testing Avraham. He wanted to see if Avraham would follow Him blindly. But God was also leading Avraham toward the fulfillment of one of the most important commandments we have: Living in Israel.

What is it that is so unique about the Land of Israel that God chose to send Avraham there?

The Vilna Gaon said that there are two commandments that a Jew fulfills with his body: sitting in the *Sukkah*, and living in Israel. It doesn't matter whether you are eating, drinking, or even sleeping in Israel, as long as your body is there. Just being in Israel is fulfilling a mitzvah.

. But what is it that makes Israel so special?

We know that certain commandments, like Shmittah (letting the land lie fallow in the seventh year), can only be performed as a mitzvah in Israel. But the Ramban goes further, explaining that even the commandments we can fulfill outside of Israel have an added dimension to them when they are performed in Israel.

It's like someone who comes into a beautiful room with the blinds drawn, in the middle of the day. He can take a flashlight or candle to light his way, but if he raises the blinds and lets the sunshine in, he will see the room in all its splendor. So, too, when someone observes the Torah in Israel, it is like letting in the sunlight. You see the beauty and wonder the land has to offer.

That's why God made Avraham leave everything and go to the land of Israel. Avraham could only reach his potential in such a land. And, even though the path was difficult and he had to overcome many obstacles, Avraham succeeded and flourished.

ויראֵ

THIS WEEK IN THE PARSHA

Three Angels Appear to Avraham

On the third day after Avraham circumcises himself, God sends three angels, disguised as humans, to visit him. Avraham runs out to greet the guests and invites them into his tent. He and his wife, Sarah, serve them a feast.

Following the meal, one of the angels tells Avraham that in exactly one year Sarah will give birth to a son. Sarah overhears this and laughs, thinking she and Avraham are too old to have children.

God asks Avraham why Sarah laughed, then assures him that the following year they will have a son. When Sarah is confronted, she is afraid, and denies laughing.

The angels leave to carry out their duties.

The Destruction of Sodom and Amorah

God tells Avraham that He has decided to destroy the people of Sodom and Amorah because of their innumerable sins. Avraham is appalled to hear that so many people will die. He feels that an injustice is being done. After all, perhaps there are some righteous people among them.

Avraham argues this point with God. Ultimately, God agrees that even if ten righteous people are found in Sodom,

He will save the entire city. But Avraham, after realizing that there are no righteous people in Sodom, understands that God's edict is just.

Meanwhile, the angels arrive at Lot's house in Sodom. The people in the city demand that Lot hand over the strangers.

Lot defends his guests only to learn that they can take care of themselves. The angels blind the people. They tell Lot that he must gather his family and leave the city at once. No one may look back once they have left the city. But as Sodom and Amorah are destroyed, Lot's wife turns back and is transformed into a pillar of salt.

Lot and his two daughters flee to the mountains to escape the destruction. Thinking they are the last people left on earth, the daughters get Lot drunk and lie with him. From this union two great nations will eventually arise, Amon and Moav.

Sarah and Avimelech

Avraham and Sarah move to Grar. Avraham fears that the people will kill him in order to take his wife, so he asks Sarah to once again pretend she is his sister. Avimelech, the king, takes Sarah for his wife, but God warns Avimelech not to touch her.

Avimelech returns Sarah to Avraham and admonishes him for not telling the truth. Avimelech then sends Avraham and Sarah away laden with gifts.

Yitzhak and Yishmael

As God promised, Sarah gives birth to Yitzhak one year later. Yitzhak is the first to be circumcised at eight days old.

Sarah sees that Yishmael is a bad influence on Yitzhak

and demands that Avraham send Hagar and her son away. Avraham at first refuses, but then relents after God tells him to listen to his wife.

The next morning, Avraham gives Hagar food and water and sends her and Yishmael out into the desert. When their water runs out, Yishmael becomes ill and Hagar, unable to bear his pitiful cries, leaves him under a bush to die. God sends an angel to Hagar to tell her that Yishmael will not die; on the contrary, he will grow to become the leader of a great nation. Hagar looks up and sees a well. She gives her son water and saves his life.

Avraham and Avimelech

Avraham accuses Avimelech and his general, Pihol, of stealing his wells. They reconcile and swear never to fight over the wells again. They call the place where they make this pact, Be'er Sheva, the well of oath.

The *Akaida:* The Binding of Yitzhak

God tells Avraham to take his only son, Yitzhak, to a mountain in the land of Moriah and sacrifice him. Without a word of protest, Avraham makes the necessary preparations and sets off on his journey. When Avraham reaches the mountain that God has shown him, he leaves his servants behind and ascends with his son.

Yitzhak asks his father, "Where is the sacrifice we are to bring to God?" and Avraham answers, "God will show us the sacrifice."

When they reach the top of the mountain, Avraham sets up

the altar and binds Yitzhak upon it. Avraham raises his knife but, just as he is about to strike, an angel calls out to Avraham and tells him not to touch Yitzhak. This was only a test from God. Avraham then sees a ram, whose horns are entangled in a nearby bush, and sacrifices it instead of Yitzhak. The angel praises Avraham and blesses him and his children.

WISDOM
OF THE
SAGES
The following Midrash shows us what a wicked place Sodom really was:

In the middle of the city, the people of Sodom placed four beds of varying lengths. When a stranger came to town, the inhabitants would tell him to lie down on any bed he liked. If the visitor chose a bed that was too short for him, the townspeople would chop off his legs so that he was exactly the size of the bed. If he chose a bed that was too long for him, six men would grab his head, arms, and legs, and stretch him until his limbs were torn apart. Is it any wonder these people were destroyed?

Sarah told Avraham to send Hagar and Yishmael away. But Avraham refused, until God told him to listen to Sarah. From this we learn that Sarah was superior to Avraham in prophecy, for she could tell that Yishmael would be a bad influence on Yitzhak, even if Avraham couldn't.

How old was Yitzhak at the time of the Akaida? Sarah gave birth to Yitzhak when she was 90 years old. She died when she was 127 years old. According to most commentators,

Sarah died of a heart attack when she heard that Yitzhak had almost been sacrificed by Avraham. Subtract 90 from 127 and you get 37. That would mean that Yitzhak was 37 years old when Avraham took him to be sacrificed.

GEMMATRIA "And behold three people are coming to him." (18:2)

The commentaries agree that the "people" referred to here were not flesh and blood, but angels. In fact, the numerical value of the Hebrew phrase *v'hinay shloshah* — "And behold three" — comes to 701. It is also the same numerical value as the phrase, "These are Mihael, Gavriel, and Refael," three well-known angels.

1. When Lot's wife looked back, she turned into a pillar of salt. Why salt? Why not turn her into a pillar of sand, or something else?

2. When Avraham arrives in Grar he asks Sarah to say she is his sister. This isn't the first time that Avraham asked Sarah to say this. It also happened in Lech Lecha (12:13). How could Avraham ask his wife to tell such a lie?

3. The Akaida is referred to as the hardest test of man. Avraham had to slaughter his son. Yitzhak had to stretch out his neck and let his father kill him. Who had the harder task? Why?

In our Parsha, we witness the most difficult test ever set before man: to take an only son and slaughter him at God's command.

What was the purpose of such a test? God knew that Avraham would sacrifice his son if He requested it. After all, God is all-knowing and does not need proof of man's loyalty or love. So why put Avraham through such mental and emotional anguish?

Perhaps the answer lies in our need to assume that our reasons for doing things are synonymous with God's reason. Why do we think that God's logic is identical to man's?

It may be that God is not testing us for His benefit, but for our own. God is actually trying to help us shape and refine ourselves by having us overcome certain personal obstacles. God knows that we can pass the test, but we must face the challenge so that *we* know we can pass the test.

When a child is born, he is born with the potential to learn the difference between right and wrong. But if he doesn't have to face any problems, then he'll never develop this ability. Whenever we have a choice and we choose good instead of evil, we not only pass the test but we become better people.

But how can a person know if he or she has the potential to pass the test?

In *Ethics of the Fathers* (3:18), Rabbi Akiva says that man is loved by God because God made man in His image. But the fact that God let man know he was created in His image shows even greater love for man. By letting us know who we are, God showed us our potential. One who is created in God's image can reach unbelievable heights. By testing us, God helps us realize our potential so that we can become better people.

We must always remember that God doesn't test someone unless he can pass the test. So, no matter how tough it may seem, if we push ourselves a bit harder, we will pass.

THE HAFTARAH CONNECTION

(Kings II 4:1)

In our Parsha, angels tell Avraham, "Just like you're alive today, you will be alive next year..."

In the Haftarah, we find the same phrase is used by the prophet Elisha. As he passed through Shunam, a woman saw him and invited him into her house. This woman, although of meager means, convinced her husband to build Elisha a room in their attic, to make the holy man more comfortable.

Elisha wanted to pay her for her kindness. He discovered that the woman wanted only one thing in life — a child. He told the woman, "Just like you're alive today, you will be alive next year, and you will embrace a child."

This story connects very well with the week's Torah reading. Not only is the prophecy similar, but the same exact phrase is used in both cases!

TELL IT WITH A SMILE

The first-grade teacher was telling her six year olds how Lot's wife turned into a pillar of salt, when one small girl chimed in, "My mother looked back once while she was driving, and she turned into a telephone pole!"

חיי שרה

Avraham Buys a Burial Place for Sarah

Sarah is 127 years old when she dies in Hevron. Avraham meets with the people of Heth and asks to purchase the burial cave known as the *Mearat Hamahpaila* – "The Cave of Pairs"– from Efron the Hitte. Efron wants to give the cave to him, but Avraham insists on paying for it. Avraham buys the cave for 400 shekels. (This cave will become the burial place of the forefathers of the Jewish nation and their wives.)

Eliezer is Sent to Look for a Wife for Yitzhak

Avraham sends his trusted servant, Eliezer, to find a wife for Yitzhak. Avraham insists that Eliezer bring the prospective bride back to Hevron; under no circumstances is Yitzhak to leave the country. Eliezer takes ten camels laden with presents, and sets out on his mission.

He arrives at his destination, Aram Naharaim, where the family of Avraham's brother lives. Instead of going into the town, he waits by the town well.

Eliezer asks God for a sign so that he might know whom to take as a wife for Yitzhak. He wants the girl to pass a test: She must draw water for him, then volunteer to draw water for his camels as well. Such a girl would be worthy of Yitzhak.

Just as he finishes outlining the test, Rivkah appears. Eliezer asks her for some water to drink. She quickly serves him and offers to water his camels as well. Eliezer is amazed and gives Rivkah presents. He wants to know who she is, and if her family can put him up. When she says that her lineage goes back to Nahor, the brother of Avraham, Eliezer knows his search is over.

Lavan, Rivkah's brother, runs out to greet them. Eliezer tells Rivkah's family why he has come and asks them to let her go to Hevron with him. Lavan and her mother want Rivkah to stay with them a little while longer, but Eliezer says he is in a hurry. They agree to leave the decision up to Rivkah. She agrees to go.

Yitzhak is out in the field praying as the camels approach. When Rivkah sees Yitzhak, she swoons. Eliezer tells her that Yitzhak is his master. Yitzhak marries Rivkah and only then is he consoled over the loss of his mother.

The Last Days of Avraham

Avraham marries Keturah. They have six children together, but Avraham decides to give all his possessions to Yitzhak. Avraham gives his other children gifts and sends them away.

Avraham is 175 years old when he dies. Yitzhak and Yishmael bury him in the Mearat Hamahpaila.

 **Sim na yadecha...** – "Please place your hand under my thigh..." (24:2)

Why did Eliezer have to place his hand under Avraham's thigh in order to swear? The numeric value of the two words *na yadecha* is 85. The Sages say that Avraham asked Eliezer to swear by his brit milah. The numerical value of milah is 85.

WISDOM OF THE SAGES

"And the life of Sarah was 100 years, and 20 years and 7 years." (23:1)

Why didn't the Torah simply say 127 years?

The Midrash says that from here we learn that Sarah was as pure from sin at 100 as she had been at 20; and she was as beautiful at 20 as she had been at 7.

Both old age and youth have advantages. Knowledge and experience come with age, while enthusiasm and energy are the signs of youth. The Torah tells us that Sarah had all the attributes of both age and youth throughout her entire life.

"And Avraham was old, coming along in days." (24:1)

The Midrash addresses the question: If Avraham was old, isn't it obvious he was coming along in days?

It seems that until that time people didn't really look their age. A person just got old and died. No one even had white hair!

Avraham and Yitzhak looked so much alike that people couldn't tell father from son. Since they both looked about the same age, showing honor for the older man became difficult to do.

Avraham asked God to help people recognize the difference between him and his son. God agreed, and told Avraham that from then on a person's physical appearance would change as he or she became older. That is why the Torah states: "Avraham was coming along in days."

"She became his wife and he loved her." (24:67)

Isn't this sentence backwards? Usually, love comes before marriage.

Yet Yitzhak first married Rivkah and only then did he love her. Even today, among certain Jewish groups, marriages are prearranged. Only after the wedding does the couple have a chance to get to know each other and fall in love.

THE HAFTARAH CONNECTION

(Kings I 1:1)

In the beginning of the Parsha, Avraham is mentioned as getting old. The rest of the Parsha deals primarily with Avraham's desire to secure the future of his lineage. When Yitzhak gets married, Avraham sends the rest of his children away. In doing so, he ensures that Yitzhak will be the sole heir to his "throne."

The Haftarah begins in the same fashion. King David is getting old. He wants to make sure that the right person will inherit the throne after he dies. One of his sons, Adoniyah, decides that he will be king when his father dies. But King David assures Bat Sheva that her son, Shlomo, will be the next Jewish king.

King David, like Avraham, wanted to make sure that the right son ruled when he died.

TABLE TALK DVAR TORAH

In the Parsha, Eliezer is faced with the problem of finding a wife for Yitzhak. But Eliezer puts the onus on God, by asking him for a sign: The first woman who agrees to give him water, and then insists on watering his camels as well, is the one for Yitzhak. And, before he knows it, Rivkah comes and fulfills the criteria precisely. Eliezer then thanks God for helping him find the right woman.

But if you look at the sign Eliezer chose, it seems a bit strange. There are many charitable women in the world. How could Eliezer rely on this test alone?

The truth is that Eliezer tests Rivkah not once, but twice in the Parsha. When he tries to take her back to Hevron, her brother and mother are reticent to let her leave right away. After Eliezer insists that it is now or never, they agree to leave the decision to Rivkah. Rivkah, a young girl, has to decide between her family and familiar surroundings, and going away to marry someone she doesn't know. Against all odds, Rivkah agrees to leave her father's house and follow Eliezer.

Rivkah's decision echoes the decisions of other great personalities in the Torah. Avraham faced such a decision when he was told by God to leave his home and head out for an unknown destination. And again, Avraham has to make a monumental decision when it comes to the Akaida — whether to go through with the sacrifice of his son. Yitzhak, too, is faced with a momentous decision: Should he allow himself to be led like a lamb to slaughter? But Avraham and Yitzhak realize that they are being tested by God and, in every case, make the right decision.

That is what Eliezer is looking for: someone who can make a difficult decision. When Rivkah hears that she will be going to marry the son of the God-fearing Avraham, she jumps at the opportunity to leave her idol-worshiping brother. So, when Rivkah agrees to come with him, Eliezer is secure in the knowledge that he, too, has made the right decision.

After all, the sign of true greatness is the ability to make the tough decisions at the right time!

1. Why was it so important for Avraham to buy Mearat Hamahpaila when Efron offered it to him for free?

2. Why was Avraham so adamant that Yitzhak only marry someone willing to live in Israel? Why couldn't Yitzhak live someplace else? Could it have something to do with the Akaida?

3. When Eliezer recounted to Lavan what had happened at the well, he changed the story a bit. Find at least two differences. What made Eliezer decide to change the story?

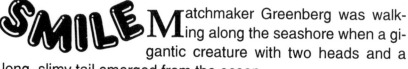

Matchmaker Greenberg was walking along the seashore when a gigantic creature with two heads and a long, slimy tail emerged from the ocean.

The matchmaker's first impulse was to run away, but then he remembered something. Conquering his fear, he ran over to the creature of the deep.

"Say," he cried, "Have I got a match for you!"

Reb Moshe saw his wife washing his pants by the stream. As he watched, she took his pants and started beating them on a flat rock with a thick branch. After a while, she took the pants, dipped them in the stream, and beat them again.

Reb Moshe uttered a silent prayer: "Thank you God for giving me a strong wife. And thank you for giving me the wisdom to get out of my pants this morning — just in time!"

תולדות

Rivkah Gives Birth to Twins

Yitzhak marries Rivkah when he is 40 years old. When it becomes clear that Rivkah is barren, Yitzhak prays for her, but it isn't until he is 60 that God hears his prayers. Rivkah becomes pregnant with twins. God tells her that each one will become a great nation, and that the older will serve the younger.

The firstborn son is called Esav, which means "already made," because he was born with a lot of hair, making him look older. The second son is called Yaacov, which means "heel," because he held onto his brother's heel as he left the womb.

Esav grows up and becomes a hunter. He is his father's favorite. Yaacov, his mother's favorite, spends his time learning.

Esav Sells his Birthright to Yaacov

Esav arrives home one day tired and hungry. Yaacov has just made lentil soup and Esav wants some. Yaacov agrees to give him the soup on condition that Esav sell him his birthright. Esav doesn't seem to care about his birthright and agrees.

Yitzhak and Avimeleh, King of the Plishtim

A terrible famine hits the land of Canaan, and Yitzhak decides to move to Grar, a city of Plishtim. God appears to him and assures him that the promise He made to Avraham will continue through Yitzhak and his descendants.

Meanwhile, Yitzhak tells everyone in Grar that Rivkah is his sister. He fears the people will kill him and take Rivkah away if he says she is his wife. But Avimeleh discovers the truth and commands the people not to touch Rivkah or harm Yitzhak.

Left alone, Yitzhak prospers and becomes very wealthy. Realizing Yitzhak is becoming powerful, Avimeleh asks him to leave. Yitzhak then moves on, redigging all the wells his father had dug, which the Plishtim had covered.

At Be'er Sheva, Yitzhak builds an altar to God. Avimeleh and his general, Pihol, go to Be'er Sheva and make a pact with Yitzhak. The king feels that God is with Yitzhak and wants his assurances that, just as he left him in peace in Grar, so, too, Yitzhak will never harm him. Yitzhak agrees.

Meanwhile, at the age of 40, Esav marries two Hitte women. This greatly troubles both Yitzhak and Rivkah.

Yaacov Receives the Firstborn's Blessing from Yitzhak

As Yitzhak becomes older, he becomes almost blind. He asks Esav to prepare a meal for him, so that he can bless him. Esav sets out to hunt an animal and serve it to his father.

Rivkah overhears Yitzhak and tells Yaacov to bring her two goats so she can prepare them for Yitzhak. She wants Yaacov to trick Yitzhak so he will receive the firstborn's blessing.

Yaacov is reluctant to do this. He reminds his mother that Esav is hairy and with one touch his father would discover the truth and then, instead of blessing him, might curse him. Rivkah assures Yaacov that any curse he receives will fall on her head.

Rivkah has a plan. She dresses Yaacov in Esav's clothing and puts the hairy skins of the goats on his hands and neck.

Yaacov then takes the food to his father. Yitzhak is surprised at the speed with which his son has prepared the food, and asks him about it. Yaacov replies that God has helped him.

Unable to see well, Yitzhak asks Yaacov to come closer so he can touch him. After Yitzhak touches him, he says, "The voice is the voice of Yaacov, but the hands are the hands of Esav." He then asks, "Are you my son, Esav?"

"Yes," Yaacov answers.

Yitzhak eats and then asks Yaacov to approach and give him a kiss. Yitzhak tells Yaacov that he smells like a field that has been blessed by God. Then Yitzhak blesses Yaacov, promising that God will give him from the dew of the heaven and the fat of the earth. People and nations will serve him. Those who bless him will be blessed and those who curse him will be cursed.

Esav Returns

Just as Yaacov leaves his father, Esav enters. Both he and Yitzhak soon realize what has happened. Esav is very angry and begs his father to give him a blessing too. At first, Yitzhak refuses, but when Esav continues pleading, Yitzhak tells him that he will live by the sword and serve his brother. However, if he humbles himself, Esav will be able to loosen the yoke of servitude from his neck.

Esav Plots to Kill Yaacov

Esav vows to kill Yaacov as soon as their father is dead. Rivkah hears of this and sends Yaacov to her brother, Lavan, in Haran. He is to stay there until she calls for him.

Yitzhak tells Yaacov to be sure to marry only someone from Lavan's household.

When Esav realizes that his father doesn't approve of his wives, he marries Mahalat, Yitzhak's niece.

WISDOM
OF THE
SAGES

"And the children moved about inside her." (25:22)

The Midrash tells us what was so special about the way the twins, Yaacov and Esav, moved around inside Rivkah. Whenever she would pass a house of idolatry, Esav would want to go out; and when she passed a house of learning, Yaacov would want to go out.

Each one wanted to be the first to exit the womb in order to become the firstborn. Eventually, Esav told Yaacov that he would kill their mother during birth unless Yaacov let him leave first! Yaacov, having no choice, gave in.

"And Yitzhak loved Esav...and Rivkah loved Yaacov." (25:28)

Why wasn't Rivkah taken in by Esav's good behavior at home? She seems to have seen through him.

In the Talmud (Tractate Yoma 9b) we learn that anyone whom the Sage Resh Lakish spoke to in the marketplace was a person you could safely do business with. Why is this only said about Resh Lakish, and not the other Sages? Because the other Sages were a bit naive about the real world and could be cheated, while Resh Lakish was a former bandit and couldn't be cheated. If he spoke to someone in the street, then that person could be trusted.

Yitzhak, having grown up in Avraham's house, could be tricked by Esav. Rivkah, who grew up with her conniving brother, Lavan, couldn't be easily tricked.

1. Why does the Torah tell us about all the wells that Yitzhak dug? It doesn't tell us how many trees he planted, or how many sheep he had.

2. Before Yitzhak was willing to bless Esav, he asked him to prepare some food. Was Yitzhak simply hungry, or is there a connection between food and a blessing?

3. Is there a way to justify what Rivkah and Yaacov did to Yitzhak and Esav?

A stingy lady owned a boarding house. For supper, the only food she would serve every day was lentil soup. She made sure that each boarder received exactly one brown lentil in his bowl.

One day, after she had served the soup, one of the boarders bent his head over the table and put his ear to the plate.

"What are you doing?" asked the woman suspiciously.

"My lentil is talking," he said.

"You don't mean it!" she exclaimed, surprise written all over her face. "What is it saying?"

"It's saying, 'Gee, I'm lonesome! I wish there were other lentils here to keep me company!'"

TABLE TALK
DVAR TORAH

A father is expected to bless his children before dying. The older child may get a special blessing, but the father is expected to bless the younger ones as well.

We know from the Parsha that Yitzhak really knew the personalities of his two sons very well. Esav was a physical person, a hunter, and Yaacov was a spiritual person, a *talmid haham*. So when he was preparing the blessings, Yitzhak made sure that each blessing was appropriate for each child.

But as it turned out, the blessing meant for Esav went to Yaacov, and the blessing meant for Yaacov went to Esav.

But if that's true, why did Yitzhak have such a hard time finding a blessing for Esav? He should have given him the blessing he had originally prepared for Yaacov.

Perhaps the answer lies in how Yitzhak perceived his sons.

Esav's blessing — the one given to Yaacov — was a very material one. The heaven and earth would work together to make him prosperous and he would rule over the other nations. Yitzhak had meant this blessing to go to Esav, since Esav was the hunter, the material one, and would appreciate it.

But the spiritual blessing Yitzhak had prepared for Yaacov wasn't appropriate for Esav. His father realized this when he heard that Esav had sold his birthright to Yaacov for a bowl of soup. Yitzhak knew that Esav would have laughed — or worse — had he heard the words his father had prepared for the *talmid haham*, the one primed to be the spiritual leader of the family.

So Yitzhak didn't know what to tell Esav. He finally came up with a weaker physical blessing — it was all that was left.

Of course, Esav wanted more, much more.

Meanwhile, Yaacov received the spiritual inheritance of his father *and* the blessing of prosperity in this world as well. That is why we Jews have a blessed share in this world and the next.

THE HAFTARAH CONNECTION

(Malahi 1:1)

In our Parsha, Yaacov manages to get the birthright from Esav, first by selling him the lentil soup and second by taking his blessing from Yitzhak. It is clear that the Torah is telling us that Yaacov is meant to be the chosen brother, carrying the legacy of Avraham and Yitzhak forward.

In our Haftarah, the prophet Malahi finds himself facing a Jewish nation that does not believe that God loves them.

What can he use as proof that God still loves His people?

Malahi recounts the story of Esav and Yaacov, telling the people that Yaacov was chosen because God saw the future of the Jewish people in him.

Indeed, the fact that the Jewish nation still exists today, even though in every generation there have been those who want to destroy us, proves that God hasn't changed His mind.

 Our Sages say that Esav used to hunt other people's livestock. They derive this from the Torah's use of the word *latzud,* which means, "to hunt." The numeric value of this word is 130.

Similarly, the words *min gezel,* which means, "from stolen goods," also have the numeric value of 130.

Angels on a Ladder

On the way to Haran to live with his uncle, Lavan, Yaacov makes camp. He takes some stones, places them around his head, and falls asleep. Then he dreams of angels going up and down a ladder. God tells Yaacov that he and his descendants will inherit the land of Canaan and that He will be with him.

When Yaacov wakes up, he realizes the sanctity of the place, and calls it Beit El, which means "The House of God."

Yaacov swears that if God will be with him, feed him, clothe him, and return him safely to his father's house, then he will give a tenth of everything he owns to God.

Yaacov Meets Rachel

Yaacov arrives at the well in Haran. The shepherds are milling around. Yaacov asks them what they are waiting for and they say they must all gather in order to push the giant rock that covers the well.

Just then, Rachel, Lavan's daughter, comes to water her father's sheep. Yaacov immediately rolls the stone off the well and helps water the flock. He then tells her who he is. Rachel tells Lavan, who runs out to meet his nephew and tells him to stay.

Lavan Tricks Yaacov

Lavan offers to pay Yaacov for working for him.

But Yaacov wants to marry Rachel in exchange for his labors.

Yaacov works for seven years. When it comes time to marry Rachel, Yaacov is tricked into marrying her older sister, Leah. Lavan then explains to Yaacov that in his village it is customary to marry off the oldest daughter first. Lavan gives Leah a servant called Zilpa.

Lavan tells Yaacov that if he agrees to work for another seven years, he may marry Rachel in a week's time. After the marriage, Lavan gives Rachel a servant called Bilha.

Rachel and Leah

Yaacov loves Rachel more than he loves Leah. But it is Leah who has the first four children: **Reuven**, which means "God has *seen* my suffering"; **Shimon**, which means "God has *heard* that I am hated"; **Levi**, which means "Now my husband will *accompany* me"; and **Yehudah**, which means "Now I will *thank* God."

Rachel is jealous of her sister. She tells Yaacov that, if she can't have children, she might as well be dead. Yaacov tells her to pray to God.

Rachel gives her maidservant, Bilha, to Yaacov. She reasons that, since Bilha is her servant, all of Bilha's children would be considered as though they had come from her. Bilha has two children; Rachel names them **Dan**, which means "God has *judged* me and seen fit to give me a son"; and **Naftali**, which means "I have *wrestled* with my sister and won."

When Leah sees that she has stopped having children, she

gives her servant, Zilpa, to Yaacov. Zilpa has two children; Leah names them **Gad**, which means "*Luck* has come"; and **Asher**, which means "Women *praise* me."

Reuven brings flowers to his mother, but Rachel wants the flowers and agrees that Yaacov will spend the night in Leah's tent in exchange for them.

Leah gives birth to three more children: **Yesahar**, which means "God has *rewarded* me"; **Zevulun**, meaning "God has given me a good *portion*"; and **Dinah**, a daughter.

God hears Rachel's prayers and grants her a child. She calls him **Yosef,** which means "May God give me *another* son."

Yaacov Leaves Lavan

Yaacov approaches Lavan and asks for permission to leave. Lavan explains that God has been very good to him since Yaacov came, and he wants him to stay. Lavan offers Yaacov some sheep he can call his own. Yaacov gets the flock rejects — the spotted lambs, dark lambs, and spotted goats. The animals multiply and soon Yaacov has a large flock of both sheep and goats.

Yaacov overhears Lavan's sons saying he "stole" from their father, and he becomes scared. God appears to Yaacov and tells him to return to his birthplace.

Yaacov explains to Rachel and Leah that they must leave now. He reminds them of the tricks Lavan played on him. Rachel and Leah agree to leave their father's house.

While Lavan is away shearing his flock, Rachel steals his idols and places them in her saddle. Yaacov decides it is time to leave and he escapes with his family.

Lavan Chases Yaacov

Lavan hears that Yaacov and his family have left and chases after them. But an angel appears and warns Lavan not to harm Yaacov. When Lavan catches up with Yaacov, he asks: Why didn't you give me the opportunity to send you off properly? And why did you steal my idols?

Yaacov explains that he did not think Lavan would let him leave. As for the idols, Yaacov insists no one from his camp stole them. Yaacov puts a curse on anyone who might have stolen the idols, not knowing it was Rachel who took them.

Lavan searches all the tents. Rachel sits on the camel in whose saddle she has hidden the idols, and Lavan doesn't find them.

Yaacov berates Lavan, telling him that if it wasn't for God's intercession, he would have left Lavan without a penny to his name, after 20 years of hard work.

Yaacov and Lavan decide to make a covenant. They erect a monument of stones, which is to be used as a boundary marker. Each person is to stay on his side of the marker. Yaacov calls the place Gal Ed, which means "pile of stones as a witness."

 What did God show Yaacov, ask the Sages, when he dreamed of the ladder and the angels?

It seems he saw a bit of the future. The word ladder, in Hebrew, *sulam*, has a numeric value of 130. The Midrash says that God showed Yaacov the mountain of Sinai, where his descendants would one day receive the Torah. The numeric value of Sinai is also 130.

TABLE TALK
DVAR TORAH

In the middle of our Parsha, the Torah inserts a seemingly unimportant story about Rachel convincing Leah to give her the flowers that her son, Reuven, had picked in the fields.

What is so important about these flowers? Why does Rachel go to such great lengths — allowing Yaacov to spend an extra night with her sister — for these flowers? If it was flowers Rachel wanted, why didn't she go out and pick them herself, or have someone else pick them for her?

The answer is part of the basic fabric of motherhood. Reuven, the oldest son, goes out into the field with the rest of the workers. He doesn't want to go home to his mother empty-handed, so he plans to surprise her with a gift of freshly picked flowers.

His mother is ecstatic. Nothing makes a mother happier than a present from her son. It's not only the gift, but the thought that is so important. And, as happy as this makes Leah, that's how sad it makes Rachel feel.

Rachel has no child of her own, no one to feel motherly pride in. So, she begs Leah to share her *nachat*, her joy. She needs the flowers. She needs to take a part in bringing Reuven up!

Leah understands this and agrees. This act of *hessed*, this kind deed, doesn't go unnoticed. She receives a great reward — two more sons, bringing her sum total to 6, exactly half of the 12 tribes.

All this helps us to see more clearly that an act of kindness never goes unnoticed by God.

1. In Yaacov's dream, he sees angels climbing up the ladder and going back down. But isn't that reversed? Shouldn't he have seen angels coming down from heaven and then going back up?

2. Rachel, the last of the four matriarchs, had a great deal of trouble having children. It seems that all our matriarchs could not conceive until God directly intervened to help them have children. Why is it that these unique women all started out childless?

THE HAFTARAH CONNECTION

(Hoshea 12:13)

In our Parsha, Yaacov succeeds in attaining power and wealth only with the intervention of God.

In our Haftarah, the prophet Hoshea uses the constant obstacles that Yaacov faced as a starting point for admonishing the Jewish people, who have begun to forget God. The people are worshiping idols and believe that their own ability has brought them wealth and power. They must learn from Yaacov that all wealth, power, and success come only from God. He is the one who took care of Yaacov, and He is the one who takes care of them.

Yaacov was able to succeed only because of God's help. This is the valuable lesson that the Jewish people forgot.

WISDOM OF THE SAGES

"I will serve you seven years for Rachel, your younger daughter." (29:18)

Why did Yaacov go into such detail? Why didn't he just say, "I will serve for Rachel" or "I will serve for your daughter Rachel"?

Lavan was a trickster. Yaacov was afraid that if he just said "Rachel," Lavan would have given him any girl named Rachel. He was also afraid to say, "your daughter Rachel," because then Lavan would have changed Leah's name to Rachel. But even with all these precautions, Lavan still managed to trick Yaacov.

The phrase, "Rachel, your younger daughter," is used in Hebrew today when someone wants to be picky or specify something in minute detail.

"And in the morning she was Leah." (29:25)

Yaacov woke up the morning after his wedding to find that he had married Leah. How could Yaacov not have known whom he married?

It seems that Yaacov suspected Lavan might try to trick him. So, he and Rachel had agreed on a secret sign that would assure him that the woman under the canopy was Rachel. But when Rachel saw that her father was determined to marry Leah to Yaacov, Rachel realized that her sister would be embarrassed in front of everyone when she failed to know the sign. Rachel revealed the secret sign to her sister, and Leah repeated the sign to Yaacov. It was only the following morning that Yaacov realized that he had been tricked.

 **haim**: Everyone knows that one shouldn't walk around without his head covered, but how can we learn this from the Torah?

Yankel: There are places in the Torah where we see this. For instance, the Torah says, "Yaacov went from Be'er Sheva to Haran."

Now I ask you Chaim, can you possibly imagine a Jew like the great patriarch Yaacov walking all that distance, in the hot sun — without a hat?

וישלח

THIS WEEK IN THE PARSHA

Yaacov Prepares to Meet Esav

Yaacov sends messengers to Esav only to discover that Esav is on his way to meet him with 400 men. Realizing there may be a battle, Yaacov splits his camp in two so that if one group is attacked, the other can flee. Then he prays to God for help. He also sends many flocks as a gift to Esav, to try to appease his brother.

Yaacov Fights an Angel

In order to keep them safe from Esav, Yaacov takes his wives and children and crosses the Yabok River. Later, when he is alone, an angel comes and fights with him throughout the night. Unable to conquer Yaacov, the angel injures Yaacov's thigh.

It is because of this injury that Jews, to this day, do not eat the *gid hanasheh* (sometimes called Jacob's sinew), the sinew that travels down the thigh of an animal.

Yaacov, however, continues the fight and refuses to let the angel go until he blesses him. The angel changes Yaacov's name to Yisrael, which means "fought with God."

Yaacov Meets Esav

Yaacov meets Esav and bows down to him. Esav gives him a big hug and a kiss, and they both cry. When Esav offers to escort Yaacov on his journey home, Yaacov tells his brother to go on without him, since the children would just slow everyone down. They part, each going his separate way.

Dinah and Shehem

Yaacov buys a piece of land in the city of Shehem. His daughter, Dinah, wanders through the city and is abducted by the son of King Hamor, who is also called Shehem. He tells his father he wants to marry Dinah.

When Yaacov's sons hear what Shehem has done to their sister, they become enraged. By this time, however, King Hamor has arrived at Yaacov's house.

The king explains that his son wants to marry Dinah. He suggests that Yaacov's sons marry the daughters of the inhabitants of Shehem. The inhabitants, in turn, will take Yaacov's daughters.

Yaacov's sons respond, hiding their true intentions. They say they agree on one condition: All males in the city must circumcise themselves. They explain that it is demeaning for a Jewish woman to marry an uncircumcised man. Shehem and Hamor call a town meeting and convince the men of the city to circumcise themselves.

On the third day after their mass circumcision, when the inhabitants of Shehem are in great pain, Shimon and Levy go into the city and kill every male. Yaacov's sons then loot the city. Yaacov rebukes them for killing all the men. He is afraid that the surrounding cities will attack the family. Shimon and Levy defend themselves, saying they will not let anyone take advantage of their sister.

Yaacov Gets a Blessing from God

God tells Yaacov to go to Beit El and build an altar. There, God officially changes Yaacov's name to Yisrael. He blesses him, saying that he should be fruitful and multiply and that a great nation will emerge from him. God promises Yaacov that He will give him the land that He promised Avraham and Yitzhak.

Rachel Gives Birth to Binyamin

Yaacov and his family leave Beit El to go to Efrat. While they are on the road, Rachel gives birth to Binyamin. Now the 12 sons of Yaacov are complete. Rachel dies in childbirth and Yaacov buries her in Beit Lehem.

Not long after, Reuven, Leah's son, takes Yaacov's bed out of Bilha's tent and moves it to his mother's tent.

Yitzhak dies in Hevron at 180 years of age. Both Yaacov and Esav bury him.

WISDOM OF THE SAGES

"Save me from the hand of my brother, from the hand of Esav." (32:12)

Yaacov prays that God will save him from Esav. But why say it twice, "my brother," and "Esav"? Certainly using either would have sufficed.

It seems Yaacov was afraid of Esav on two counts. First, he was afraid of killing his brother, or being killed by him. And second, if Esav ended up signing a treaty with him, Yaacov was afraid that Esav would exert a great deal of influence on him and his family.

That is why he asked God to save him "from the hand of my brother" — from coming under the hand, under the influence of Esav; and "from Esav" — from the bloodshed that follows Esav wherever he goes. God listened to Yaacov's prayers, and Esav returned the same day.

"**And Yaacov asked the angel, Please tell me your name, and he (the angel) said, Why do you ask me my name?**" (32:30)

Our Sages say that the angel that fought with Yaacov was Esav's guardian angel. This angel is a metaphor for the evil inclination that is in everyone. The angel didn't want to tell Yaacov its name, because the more you know about the evil inclination the more you can protect yourself from it. Once you start asking questions, the evil inclination loses its mysteriousness, and thereby its power.

"**And Esav said, I have much.**" (33:9)
"**And Yaacov said...I have everything.**"(33:10-11)

These statements sum up the basic difference between the two brothers. Esav's comment indicates that, although he has plenty, he still wants more. Yaacov, on the other hand, is satisfied with what he has.

GEMMATRIA

"**With Lavan have I lived.**" (32:5)

The gemmatria of the Hebrew word *garte,* which means, "I lived," is 613.

The number 613 was a hint to Esav that, although Yaacov lived with the trickster Lavan for a long time, he still kept all 613 mitzvot.

TABLE TALK
DVAR TORAH

Yaacov was all alone on one side of the Yabok River, while the rest of his family was on the other side. Suddenly, someone appears and starts to fight with him. It turns out that this "someone" is actually a something. The Sages explain that it was actually Esav's angel who picked the fight with Yaacov. After a battle that takes almost all night, the angel accepts the fact that he cannot win and, in effect, declares Yaacov the champion.

But was Yaacov really the winner? If we look at the immediate results of the battle, Yaacov seems to have lost. After all, he will be limping for the rest of his life, while the angel is no worse off than before!

The Maggid of Minsk explains what happened:

The winner and loser of a battle can only be decided once you know what the fight is about. For example, in a boxing match, the winner and loser of the match can be easily decided. The person who remains standing at the end of the match (or the one to score the most points) is the winner.

However, in this case, the fight was not purely a physical one; it was also an ideological fight between the forces of purity and light — Yaacov — and the forces of impurity and darkness — Esav's angel.

On another level, their fight was one of words and ideas. When two people are having a debate and one gets up and smacks the other, then the one doing the hitting obviously feels his argument is not good enough to defeat his opponent; he had to resort to violence.

The same is true here. The very fact that the angel had to maim Yaacov shows us that he realized his ideology couldn't convince Yaacov. Yaacov is therefore the real winner. His ideology triumphs.

The very fact that we are commanded not to eat the sinew that was ripped by Esav's angel serves as a reminder that in the battle against the forces of Esav, we are on the winning side.

1. Before the incident with Dinah, the Torah tells us that Yaacov bought land in Shehem for 100 kesita. Why does the Torah tell us that he bought a piece of land? After all, not all of our patriarchs' business ventures are listed in the Torah.

2. Rachel was Yaacov's most beloved wife. Yet, when she dies, he buries her on the side of a road. Why didn't he bury her in the Mearat Hamahpaila, with the other matriarchs?

3. In chapter 36, verse 6, when Esav went to find a place to live, he took his wives and children — in that order. Compare this to chapter 31, verse 17, where Yaacov reverses the order. What difference does the order make?

Yaacov had to prepare himself to fight Esav's army. But not every army is filled with gung-ho heroes. Here is one of the dialogues that might have taken place as Yaacov gave his men a pep talk.

"This is it men! Esav and 400 soldiers are coming our way. Get your swords ready. It looks like we're in for some serious hand-to-hand combat!"

Private Benjamin raises his hand.

"Yes, private, what is it?"

"General Yaacov," replies the scared private. "Does that mean we'll be fighting man-to-man?"

"Hand-to-hand, man-to-man, it's all the same," answers Yaacov.

"Well then," Private Benjamin pleads, "how about showing me my man? Maybe he and I can work this thing out by ourselves?!"

THE HAFTARAH CONNECTION

(Ovadiah 1:1)

In our Parsha, Esav takes a small army to meet Yaacov. Yaacov prepares to meet his older brother and hopes to triumph, just as he had triumphed by receiving the blessings of the firstborn.

Esav went on to become the father of a great nation, Edom. The Edomites, true to the blessing given by Yitzhak, lived by their sword. And, in so doing, oppressed the Jews.

In our Haftarah, Ovadiah the prophet foretells what will be Edom's fate. Ovadiah himself was an Edomite who converted to Judaism. He warns his former nation that just as Yaacov triumphed over Esav, the Jews, with the help of God, will eventually triumph over Edom.

וישב

THIS WEEK IN THE PARSHA

Yosef and the Coat of Many Colors

At 17, Yosef is a shepherd just like his brothers. He is also a gossiper, telling his father about his brothers' exploits. Yaacov favors Yosef over his other sons because Yosef is the son of his old age. Yaacov even makes Yosef a beautiful coat of many colors. Yosef's brothers are jealous and they resent him.

Yosef's Two Dreams

Yosef dreams about 12 bushels of wheat. Suddenly, Yosef's bushel rises up and the other bushels bow down to it. When he repeats the dream to his brothers, they jeer at him and ask him if he really believes they will ever bow down to him. The brothers hate him even more as a result of the dream.

Yosef has another dream in which the sun, moon, and 11 stars are bowing down to him. When he repeats this dream, his father scolds him, saying, "Will I, your mother, and your brothers bow down to you?"

Yosef is Sold into Slavery

Yosef's brothers tend their father's flock near Shehem. Yaacov sends Yosef to go see how they are doing. When his brothers see him coming, they plot to kill him. Reuven, the oldest brother, suggests that instead of killing him, they throw him into a pit. That way they won't actually kill him. Reuven's secret intention is to sneak back and save Yosef.

When Yosef reaches his brothers, they take off his coat and throw him into a pit. Then they sit down to eat. When a caravan of Yishmaelites arrives, Yehudah says they should sell Yosef instead of leaving him to die. The brothers sell Yosef for twenty pieces of silver. Then they tear Yosef's coat, dip it in goat's blood, and give it to their father. When Yaacov sees the blood, he assumes that a wild animal has killed Yosef. He mourns for him for many days, and refuses to be consoled.

Meanwhile, Yosef is resold to a caravan of Midyanites, who bring him to Egypt. There he is sold to Potifar, Pharaoh's chief butcher.

Yehudah and Tamar

Yehudah leaves his brothers and marries a Canaanite woman. They have three sons: Air, Onan, and Shayla. Yehudah finds a wife for Air, called Tamar. Air does evil things, and God kills him. Yehudah then has Onan marry Tamar. Onan knows that any child that will come out of this union will be considered Air's, so he won't let her become pregnant. God kills Onan as well.

Yehudah tells Tamar to return to her father's house until Shayla will be old enough to marry her.

A long time later, Yehudah's wife dies and, after mourning

her, he goes to Timna to shear his sheep.

Tamar realizes that even though Shayla is old enough to marry her, Yehudah will not allow it. So, she puts on a veil and stands by the road to Timna, waiting for Yehudah. Yehudah does not recognize her and thinks she is a prostitute. He says he will pay her with some goats. However, since he doesn't have any goats with him, he agrees to leave his signet ring, cord, and staff with her as security. Later, when Yehudah sends the goats to her in order to get back his possessions, she has disappeared.

About three months later, Yehudah hears that Tamar is pregnant. He condemns her to death. But before the sentence can be carried out, she produces his ring, cord, and staff. He realizes that she is in the right since he did not give her his son, Shayla, and sets her free.

Tamar gives birth to twins: Peretz and Zerah.

Yosef's Road to Greatness

Meanwhile, in Egypt, Potifar sees that Yosef is successful in everything that he does and puts him in charge of his estate. Potifar's wife sees how handsome Yosef is and tries to seduce him. When Yosef refuses her advances she claims he attacked her and Potifar has him thrown into jail.

God is with Yosef and the jail warden puts Yosef in charge of the other prisoners.

The Pharaoh's butler and baker are in jail. One night, each has a dream, which Yosef interprets for them. The butler dreams that he has three clusters of ripe grapes, which he squeezes into a cup and gives to Pharaoh. Yosef tells him that the three clusters represent three days. In three days, Pharaoh is going to give the butler his job back. Yosef asks the butler to remember to get him out of jail, after he is freed.

The baker dreams that there are three baskets on top of his head. In the uppermost one are all kinds of food that Pharaoh likes to eat. Birds come and eat from that basket. Yosef interprets the dream, saying that in three days Pharaoh is going to hang the baker.

Three days later, on Pharaoh's birthday, the butler receives his old job back and the baker is hung. The butler, however, forgets all about Yosef.

WISDOM
OF THE
SAGES
"And the pit was empty, it had no water." (37:24)

Our Sages ask: If the pit that Yosef was thrown into was empty, doesn't that mean there was no water?

In tractate Shabbat, the Talmud indicates that while the pit had "no water," it was full of snakes and scorpions.

We learn from the wording of the verse that just like the Torah hints at the negative feature of the well, i.e., that it was empty of water but full of snakes and scorpions, we, too, should accent the positive traits of people and only hint at their negative traits.

"In three more days, Pharaoh will hang you." (40:19)

Why did Yosef interpret the baker's dream in such an abrupt and negative way?

A story is told of a famous artist who drew a lifelike portrait of a man with a basket of fruit on his head. The fruit looked so real that birds would try to eat it. A prize was announced for anyone who could find something wrong with the painting. A wise man said that the painting had a major flaw. The man was obviously not lifelike, for had the man looked as real as the fruit, the birds would have been too scared to eat from his basket!

Yosef realized that the baker had seen himself as someone dead, otherwise the birds wouldn't have eaten the bread in the basket.

1. The Torah says that Yaacov favored Yosef because he was the child of his old age. But we know that Yosef wasn't the youngest son, Binyamin was. According to the Torah, Yaacov should have loved Binyamin even more than Yosef! Why then was Yosef the most loved?

2. The focal point of this Parsha is the selling of Yosef into slavery. Why, in the middle of all the action, does the Torah insert the story of Yehudah and Tamar? Couldn't that story have been presented at a more appropriate time?

3. Yosef asked Pharaoh's butler not to forget him. Our Parsha ends with the verse, "And the butler did not remember Yosef, and he forgot him." Was this forgetfulness ingratitude, an accident, or divine intervention?

GEMMATRIA

"And Yaacov lived in the dwelling place of his father..." (37:1)

Where exactly was this dwelling place? The gemmatria for the phrase *migurey aviv*, "the dwelling place of his father," is 278.

The gemmatria gives us a hint that it was Hevron, for the numeric value of *ze Hevron*, "This is Hevron," is also 278.

TABLE TALK
DVAR TORAH

The beginning of the Parsha highlights some of the animosity that existed between Yosef and his brothers.

The Torah says, "And he brought their evil talk to their father." (37:2) One of the reasons the brothers disliked Yosef was because he would say bad things about them to their father.

The commentaries ask, How could such a righteous man as Yosef sin by gossiping about his brothers, speaking *lashon harah*?

Some Sages say that Yosef didn't actually gossip about his brothers. Rather, Yaacov used Yosef as a model for his brothers to follow. He would lecture them, demanding that they follow Yosef's example. This set up a poor relationship between Yosef and his brothers; they felt that being so good was his way of making them look bad.

However, other Sages feel that even a righteous man like Yosef might have been caught within the web of lashon harah. After all, there are so many laws relating to lashon harah that it's practically impossible not to transgress this sin.

The great Rabbi Yisrael Meir Hakohen, also known as the Hafetz Hayim, refrained from all gossip. He said that lashon harah is more dangerous than any gun or bomb made by man because while all weapons have a specific range in which they work, lashon harah can cause damage to anyone, anywhere in the world. You can ruin a man's life and reputation — in effect, destroy him — just by speaking evil about him.

Once the Hafetz Hayim was traveling in a carriage with a few other passengers. One of the passengers, who didn't recognize him, asked if he had heard about the great Hafetz Hayim. The Hafetz Hayim, being a modest man, answered that he knew of the man, but didn't think that he was all that great. Upon hearing this, the passenger smacked the Hafetz Hayim across the face.

The Hafetz Hayim said that he learned from this episode that lashon harah is so bad that a person may not even speak lashon harah about himself!

THE HAFTARAH CONNECTION

(Amos 2:6)

In this week's Parsha, the brothers sell Yosef into slavery.

In the Haftarah, the prophet Amos tells the nation that even though they bring sacrifices and celebrate Holy Days, God is going to punish them and exile them. One of the reasons for this severe punishment is that the people are "selling the righteous for money." This is the same sin that the brothers committed against Yosef.

Being dutiful to God is not enough, says the prophet. You must also be dutiful to your fellow man.

TELL IT WITH A SMILE

Yosef had a dream that the sun, moon, and stars all bowed down to him. This opens a philosophical debate as to which of these creations of God is more important. The Sages of Chelm had their own way of solving this question.

"Which is more important, the sun or the moon?" a citizen of Chelm asked the Rabbi.

"What a silly question!" snapped the Rabbi. "The moon, of course! It shines at night when we really need it. But who needs the sun to shine when it's already broad daylight?"

מקץ

THIS WEEK IN THE PARSHA

Pharaoh's Dreams

Two years after Yosef is sent to prison, Pharaoh has two dreams. In the first one, seven fat and healthy cows come out of the river to graze in the meadow. Then seven thin and scrawny cows emerge from the river. The seven thin cows eat the seven fat cows, but become no fatter.

In the second dream, seven healthy ears of corn grow on one stalk, and seven sickly ears of corn grow on another. The sickly ears of corn devour the healthy ones.

Pharaoh is very disturbed by his dreams, especially since none of his advisors can interpret them. The chief butler tells Pharaoh that when he was in jail, there was a young Jewish slave who interpreted his dream correctly. Pharaoh summons Yosef, who tells him that God is the one who truly interprets the dreams. Yosef then explains that both dreams mean there will be seven years of plenty in Egypt followed by seven years of famine. The seven years of famine will be so severe that they will erase all memory of the years of plenty.

Yosef's New Name

Pharaoh is so impressed with Yosef that he makes him his second-in-command. He also gives Yosef a new name, Tsof-nat Panayah, which means "Interpreter of Secrets," and marries him off to Asnat. They have two sons. The first is called

Menashe, because "God has made me *forget* all my troubles." The second son is called **Efraim**, because "God has made me *blossom* in the land of my affliction."

Yosef Meets his Brothers

As Yosef had predicted, after the seven years of plenty, the seven years of famine are indeed very difficult. All those who want food must come to Yosef. People from surrounding countries must also come to Egypt for food.

Yaacov also suffers from the famine. He sends all of his sons, except Binyamin, to buy food in Egypt.

When Yosef's brothers arrive in Egypt, they are brought before Yosef and bow down to him. They don't recognize Yosef, but he recognizes them. Yosef remembers the dream he had of his brothers bowing down to him.

Yosef and Binyamin

Yosef accuses his brothers of being spies. In defending themselves, they tell him that they were once 12 brothers but one is missing and one is at home.

Yosef locks his brothers up for three days. On the third day, he tells them that to prove they are telling the truth, they must bring their youngest brother to him.

While in front of Yosef, Reuven reminds his brothers that he had told them not to harm Yosef, but they had not listened. The brothers realize that God is punishing them. When Yosef hears how badly they feel, he is so overcome with emotion he has to leave the room.

Nevertheless, to make sure they return, Yosef locks Shimon in jail as a hostage.

Before the brothers leave, Yosef tells his servant to secretly replace the money the brothers used to buy food, into their saddle bags. On the way home, the brothers discover the money and are scared, not knowing what may happen to them.

When the brothers return home they tell their father what has happened. Yaacov refuses to let them take Binyamin. Reuven tells Yaacov that he can kill his own two sons — Yaacov's grandchildren — if he fails to bring Binyamin back! It is only when their food runs out and Yehudah promises to be responsible for Binyamin that Yaacov finally relents.

The brothers return to Egypt. When Yosef sees his brothers, he asks them about their father. He gives them all presents, but Binyamin is given five times as many presents as the others.

Once again, Yosef tells his servant to secretly replace the brothers' money into their saddle bags. In addition, he is to place Yosef's special silver goblet into Binyamin's bag. When the brothers leave, Yosef sends his servant to chase after them. When he catches up to the brothers, he finds the goblet in Binyamin's saddle bag.

The brothers are brought before Yosef. Yehudah tells Yosef that they have no excuse, and they will all become his slaves. Yosef tells them that only the guilty one will serve him and the rest are free to go.

WISDOM
OF THE
SAGES

"And the second child Yosef called Efraim, for God has made me blossom in the land of my affliction." (41:52)

Why does Yosef refer to Egypt in this manner? Egypt is called "the garden of God," a land that has everything. Doesn't

Yosef's remark smack of ingratitude to his adopted home? After all, Yosef had risen to a position of great power and wealth in Egypt.

Yosef refers to Egypt as "the land of my affliction" because even the most comfortable exile is still an affliction.

"And Egypt became starved and the people cried out to Pharaoh for bread and he said to them, 'Go to Yosef and do whatever he tells you to do.'"(41:55)

Rashi explains that Yosef instructed the Egyptians to circumcise themselves before he would supply them with food.

The Sfat Emet is of the opinion that Yosef was wrong in forcing them to circumcise themselves. Yosef should have been tolerant even of those who represented the exact opposite of the values he stood for.

1. Why didn't Yosef reveal his true identity right away, when he realized his brothers didn't recognize him? Did he have a noble reason in mind, or was he trying to take revenge?

2. Yosef keeps one of the brothers as a prisoner to make sure that the others will return with Binyamin. Why does he pick Shimon to be the prisoner?

3. When Reuven tries to convince his father to let Binyamin go with them, he tells his father he can kill his two sons, Yaacov's grandchildren, if Binyamin does not return. Yaacov refuses this offer. However, when Yehudah says that he guarantees that Binyamin will be brought back safely, Yaacov agrees. Besides the need for food, what prompted Yaacov to accept Yehudah's offer over Reuven's?

TABLE TALK
DVAR TORAH

The Midrash tells us that Yosef consistently put his faith in God. He was always sure that God would help him.

But then we read a Midrash that tells us Yosef spent two years in jail because he depended on the butler to get him out of jail. This, according to the Midrash, was a breach of faith. Yosef should have asked God, not the butler, for help.

It seems as if these Midrashim are praising and reprimanding Yosef for the same thing — faith in God.

This apparent contradiction is resolved when we understand that Yosef trusted in God, but, at the same time, wanted to do something to help himself out of his dire situation. For ordinary people this attempt to remedy a bad situation is quite normal, and appropriate. We should not wait around for miracles to happen.

The following story illustrates this point.

A man was on a sinking ship. While everyone was jumping into the lifeboats, he waited, certain that God would save him.

The Coast Guard arrived and rescued all the other passengers, but the man waved them away, secure in his knowledge that God would save him. Unfortunately, after refusing everyone's help, he drowned.

When the man appeared before God, he asked God why He hadn't saved him. "After all," he said to God, "I depended on You, and You alone."

"That's fine," God answered. "But when I sent the Coast Guard to rescue you, you refused to be saved!"

People must trust in God but also help themselves. But what if you see God's hand helping you? Do you make your own plans just in case God's plan doesn't work fast enough?

Yosef saw clearly that God was manipulating events to get him to a certain point in life. Yet Yosef decided to ask the butler for help, just in case. It was a backup plan.

But we see that when the butler does mention Yosef to Pharaoh, he doesn't mention the promise he made to Yosef. This shows us that God designated the time and place for the butler to remember Yosef. It was not Yosef's plan, but God's plan that saved Yosef. That is why Yosef was punished for what he did, and had to wait two years to be rescued. Indeed, Yosef accepted his punishment and regretted what he had done.

GEMMATRIA In many editions of the Bible, at the end of each Parsha you can find a record of the number of verses in that Parsha. Meketz is the only Parsha where the number of words — 2,025 — and the number of verses are listed. What is the reason for this?

The B'nai Yisashar points out that Meketz is almost always read on the Shabbat of Hanukkah. The symbol of Hanukkah is the candle, which in Hebrew is called *ner*. The numerical value of ner is 250. Multiply the 250 by the number of days of Hanukkah, 8, and you get 2,000. Hanukkah always falls out on the 25th day of the Hebrew month of Kislev. Add 25 to the 2,000 and you have 2,025, the exact number of words in the Parsha.

TELL IT WITH A SMILE Joe walked into synagogue during the Torah reading of Meketz. Being an uneducated Jew, he asked someone to explain the events. Simon gladly volunteered and filled him in on what was happening to Yosef. Hearing all the troubles that befell Yosef, Joe began to cry.

Exactly one year later, Joe walked into the same synagogue

at the same time and asked Simon to tell him what was going on. Simon repeated what he had said the previous year. To his amazement, Joe started laughing hysterically.

"Why are you laughing like a fool?" Simon asked, annoyed.

"Well, you would think," Joe answered, still laughing, "that after what happened to him last year, Yosef would have learned his lesson. Instead he gets into the same fix again!"

THE HAFTARAH CONNECTION

(Kings I 3:15)

In both the Parsha and Haftarah, the kings have a dream. In the Parsha, Pharaoh has a dream concerning the future of his people.

In our Haftarah, God appears to King Solomon in his dream and grants him one wish. The king requests that which will help him serve his people better — wisdom.

Both Pharaoh and Solomon, upon awakening, realize that their dream is more than just a dream — it is something sent from heaven.

וַיִּגַּשׁ

THIS WEEK IN THE PARSHA

Yosef Reveals his True Identity to his Brothers

When it becomes clear that Yosef is determined to keep Binyamin prisoner, Yehudah steps forward and offers himself in exchange for his younger brother. Yehudah explains that he is responsible for Binyamin and that his father will surely die if Binyamin fails to return home.

Yosef is unable to control his emotions any longer. He starts to cry, and reveals his true identity to his brothers. He wants to know all about his father, Yaacov, but the brothers are too shocked to answer him. Yosef tells them not to be afraid. He explains that God has set up this situation to make sure that Yaacov and his family would not starve during the famine. He tells them to bring his father to Egypt since the famine will last another five years. He then kisses them.

When Pharaoh discovers that Yosef's brothers are in Egypt, he tells them to bring their families to Egypt.

Yaacov Travels to Egypt

When the brothers arrive in Canaan, they tell their father the good news, but Yaacov finds it hard to believe. It is only after they recount everything Yosef told them to say, and show him the presents from Yosef, that Yaacov believes them.

Yaacov takes his family and all of their possessions and sets out for Egypt. On the way, he stops at Be'er Sheva and offers a sacrifice to God.

God appears to him in a dream and tells him not to be afraid. God promises to go with him to Egypt and return him to his homeland. God also promises that Yaacov's children will become a great nation in Egypt. Yaacov awakens, gathers his family, and continues on his way. In all, Yaacov's family consists of 70 members when they enter Egypt.

Yosef is Reunited with his Father

Yaacov sends Yehudah to Goshen, a fertile area in Egypt, to survey the land. Yosef comes to greet his father, hugs him, and begins to cry. Yaacov declares that now he is ready to die.

Yosef coaches his brothers to say they are shepherds when they speak to Pharaoh. Since the Egyptians hate shepherds, Pharaoh will make sure they are separated from the rest of the nation. In this way, the brothers will be able to lead their own lives.

The plan works. When he hears what the brothers have to say, Pharaoh tells Yosef to settle his brothers anywhere he wants.

Yosef then brings Yaacov in front of Pharaoh. When asked his age, Yaacov says that he is 130 years old. But, he adds, the years have been few and unhappy ones; he hasn't even reached the age of his forefathers. Yaacov then blesses Pharaoh.

Yosef the Provider

Yosef gives his family an estate in Ramses, one of the best areas in the land of Goshen, and makes sure they have enough to eat during the years of famine.

The Egyptians, however, suffer greatly. Yosef sells them food and collects their money for Pharaoh's treasury. A year later, the people come for food again, but this time they have no money. Yosef agrees to barter food for their cattle. The following year the people clamor for food, and this time Yosef gives them food in exchange for their land.

Eventually, Yosef buys almost all the land in Egypt for Pharaoh. He then makes the people move from one end of Egypt to the other. The only people left owning land in Egypt are the priests. Pharaoh makes sure they have food, so they won't have to sell their land.

Yosef hands out seeds to everyone. They are to plant the seeds and give one-fifth of their produce to Pharaoh; the rest they may keep for themselves. The Egyptians are very thankful to Yosef for keeping them alive.

Yisrael (Yaacov) and his family continue to live in Egypt, in the land of Goshen, where they prosper and multiply.

TELL IT WITH A SMILE

An elderly Jewish woman boarded a train and sat down opposite a man. After looking at him for a few minutes, she asked him if he was Jewish.

He looked at her strangely and politely answered that he wasn't. A few minutes later, the woman again asked him if he was Jewish. The man replied again that he most definitely was not. Some time later the woman asked him a third time if he was sure he wasn't Jewish.

The man said, "Listen lady, if it will make you stop asking me, yes, I'm Jewish."

The lady looked at him intently and said, "That's funny, you don't look Jewish."

WISDOM OF THE SAGES

"And Yosef told his brothers, 'I am Yosef,' and his brothers couldn't answer him, because they feared him." (45:3)

According to the Midrash, the brothers were so strong they could have destroyed all of Egypt. Why, then, were they afraid of Yosef?

The brothers were only strong when the truth was on their side. When Yosef told them who he was, they realized the magnitude of their sin and that the truth was with Yosef. The brothers weren't afraid of Yosef, but rather the truth that he represented.

"And behold your eyes see...that it is my mouth that talks to you." (45:12)

Rashi says that Yosef proved who he was by speaking Hebrew. After all, the brothers didn't recognize him because he had grown a beard and he spoke to them through an interpreter. Now he was speaking to them directly, in the language that they knew, Hebrew, so they should be able to recognize his voice.

"And Yaacov said, few and bad have been the days of my life, and they haven't reached..." (47:9)

For speaking badly about his life, Yaacov was punished. Yitzhak lived to be 180 years old. Yaacov lived to be 147, 33 years less than his father.

If we count up the words in the two verses in which Yaacov complains to Pharaoh, we find that there are exactly 33 words. Yaacov lost one year for every word of complaint.

TABLE TALK
DVAR TORAH

At the end of the Parsha we are given an accounting of how the Egyptian economy was sustained during the years of famine. While this information is interesting, it is difficult to understand why the Torah insists we know what happened to the Egyptians. Isn't it enough to know that Yosef saved them, and, at the same time, provided for his family?

Actually, it is very important for us to know the details of what happened to the Egyptians so that we can better appreciate what God did for us when we became His nation.

The Egyptians sold themselves and their land to Yosef in return for food. The land became Pharaoh's property. He could, as Yosef did, move them about at his will, since they no longer owned anything.

In Jewish law, land in Israel could not be sold to someone indefinitely. No king or ruler could shift a family out of their land forever. "And the land shall no be sold forever, for the land belongs to Me." (Vayikra 25:23) Even if a person was forced to sell his land in time of need, they knew that eventually they would get it back. That is a command in the Torah. It gives people a permanent hold on a piece of the land and makes it all the more dear to them.

The same is true regarding people. In Egypt, a slave was dependent on his master's whim. He could do whatever he wanted to him. He could keep the slave in chains or set him free. But a Jewish slave was different: "For they are My slaves... they can't be sold like other slaves." (Vayikra 25:42) A Jewish slave had rights, and he knew that eventually he would be set free.

We also find that in Egypt, the priests didn't sell their land to Yosef. The Pharaoh made sure they kept their land and had enough food at all times.

In Jewish law, the Kohanim don't even own land! No king or ruler can control them. They are dedicated to God. It is the people's obligation to make sure that the Kohanim have food and are taken care of. In return, the Kohanim help the people get closer to God, thereby creating a symbiotic relationship.

The Torah shows us what life is like when a nation is not under the umbrella of God. The Egyptians were at the mercy of men, at the whim of masters who might or might not decide to treat them fairly and with dignity. The Jews who entered the land of Israel entered with the Torah, the guidebook not only for spiritual prosperity but for economic prosperity and well-being, as well.

THE HAFTARAH CONNECTION

(Yehezkel 37:15)

Our Parsha begins with Yehudah stepping forward to speak to Yosef. He is willing to be Yosef's slave. This completes the circle started when Yehudah stepped forward to tell the brothers to sell Yosef.

In the Haftarah, the prophet Yehezkel is told by God to prepare two pieces of wood. On one piece he is to write "Yehudah," and on the other, "Efraim" (Yosef's son). God tells him to put the two pieces together in his hand. When he does so, they become one piece of wood.

God was essentially telling the prophet that by taking Yehudah and Efraim and placing them together, God would unite the Jewish people and end the exile.

The Jews went to Egypt because Yehudah and Yosef weren't united. Now, God was going to unite the two in the land of Israel.

1. The Torah mentions that, at a certain point, Yosef couldn't hold back, and he had to reveal his true identity to his brothers. What forced him to reveal his identity? After all, he had already waited 17 years!

2. When Yosef bought the Egyptians' land, he made them move to different cities. Everyone actually became a stranger in his own land. Why did Yosef do this?

When Pharaoh spoke to Yosef, he told him to settle his brothers *bemaytav ha'aretz*, "in the best of the land." (47:11)

The numerical value of these words is 359.

Where did they live? In the land of Goshen, which also has the numeric value of 359.

ויחי

THIS WEEK IN THE PARSHA

Yaacov Blesses Yosef's Sons

Yaacov lives in Egypt for 17 years. When he reaches 147 years old, he realizes he will soon die and asks Yosef to promise to bury him with his forefathers.

When Yosef realizes his father is very ill, he brings his two sons, Menashe and Efraim, to be blessed by Yaacov. Yaacov tells Yosef that Menashe and Efraim will be like his own children — each will become a tribe when Yosef dies.

Yaacov has trouble seeing, and when Yosef brings his two sons to him, Yaacov asks, "Who are they?" Yosef explains that they are his sons, and Yaacov asks that they be brought closer. He hugs and kisses them. Then Yosef stands the two boys in front of their grandfather in preparation for the blessing. Menashe stands on Yaacov's right, and Efraim on his left. But Yaacov does a strange thing: He puts his right hand on Efraim and his left hand on Menashe.

First, Yaacov blesses Yosef, saying, "The God before whom my fathers have conducted themselves, the God who has been my shepherd throughout my whole life until this day, the angel who helped me overcome evil should bless these boys in my name and the name of Avraham and Yitzhak, and they should grow in number like the fish of the sea."

Yosef sees that his father's hands are crossed, the right hand on Efraim and the left on Menashe, and he tries to switch them. Yaacov says that he knows Menashe is older, but Efraim, the younger brother, will become the greater of the two. He blesses them, saying, "All those who bless their children will say, 'May God make you as Efraim and Menashe.'"

Yaacov assures Yosef that God will bring them to the land of Israel. He then calls in the rest of his children and tells them what will be in the end of days.

Yaacov blesses each of his children, describing their characteristics.

Yosef's Brothers Fear for their Lives

After the blessings, Yaacov tell his sons to bury him in Mearat Hamahpaila.

Yaacov dies and is embalmed. All of Egypt mourns him for 70 days. Yosef leads a large entourage to bury his father and the family mourns their father for an additional seven days.

After they bury Yaacov, the brothers fear that Yosef will want to take revenge on them for what they did to him when he was young. They go to him and say that their father left a last message for Yosef, requesting that he forgive them for having sold him into slavery.

Yosef cries when he hears this. The brothers offer themselves to him as slaves. Yosef tells them that they have nothing to fear. God put him in this position of authority. They may have wanted to harm him, but God changed their harmful actions into something good. Yosef assures them that he will continue to provide for their families. The brothers are comforted by these words.

Yosef makes his brothers promise to take his bones with them when they leave Egypt. He dies at 110 years old and is embalmed and buried in Egypt.

WISDOM OF THE SAGES

The Midrash says that until the day Yaacov became ill, no one ever got sick before they died. They just sneezed, and their soul would leave them. Perhaps this explains why even today, when someone sneezes, many people say, "God bless you!"

Yaacov told God that he wanted to know when he was going to die so that he could bless his children. So he asked God to change the order of things so that a person would get sick before he died. God agreed, and Yaacov became the first person to get sick before dying.

"Do me a kindness and truth, please do not bury me in Egypt." (47:29)

Why did Yaacov consider his sons' burying him out of Egypt a "kindness and truth"?

Our Rabbis explain that when you do a favor for a living person, somewhere in the back of your mind you may have ulterior motives. Perhaps the person will one day be able to repay the favor. So what you are doing may be a kindness, but it is not grounded in absolute truth.

However, when you do a favor for the dead, you know you will not get anything in return. You do the deed without any ulterior motives.

That's why Yaacov considered the willingness of his children to bury him in Israel not only a kindness but also an absolute truth, an act of honor and allegiance to their father.

"Zevulun will live by the seas, Yesahar is an agile beast of burden." (49:13-14)

In the blessings given by Yaacov to these two sons we see

how the relationship between the tribe of Zevulun — the merchants — and the tribe of Yesahar — the scholars — became a case of brotherly symbiosis. Zevulun's descendants supported Yesahar's descendants so that the latter could learn without worrying about how to make a living.

God knows that not everyone can sit and learn all day. The tribe of Zevulun was better at making a living than at learning, while the tribe of Yesahar was better at studying than at working in the marketplace. Together, they were an unbeatable team. From this we learn that if, for one reason or another, it is hard to sit and learn Torah, you can still share in the mitzvah of learning by helping to support one who learns.

 **1. Why did Yaacov choose Yosef's children to be separate tribes, and not Reuven's? After all, Reuven was the firstborn.**

2. When mentioning the last day of Yaacov's life, the Torah says, "He was dying, and was gathered into his people." (49:33) But the Torah does not say he died. Why isn't the word death used with Yaacov? Can it have something to do with the fact that he fathered the Twelve Tribes?

 When Yaacov blesses Shimon and Levi, he says, *ki biapam hargu ish*, "for in their fury they have killed a man."

The gemmatria of this phrase is 678. Yaacov does not mention the name of the man they killed, but remember, Shimon and Levi were the ones who destroyed Shehem. The words *ze Shehem ben Hamor*, "this is Shehem the son of Hamor," also have the numeric value of 678. So it is logical to assume that Yaacov is referring to Shehem, the one who defiled Dinah.

TABLE TALK
DVAR TORAH

This week's Parsha is full of blessings. But the first to be blessed are Yosef's children, Efraim and Menashe. These two are the only grandchildren of Yaacov to be included as separate tribes of Israel.

And yet, within the story of the blessing, we see that Yaacov seems to make the same mistake he made years earlier with Yosef, his favorite son. At that time Yaacov played favorites, and the results were disastrous. Yosef's brothers hated him and banded together to destroy him. By now, Yaacov must have known what had happened, but he still persists in committing the same error again. Instead of blessing Menashe, the oldest son, he gives the younger son, Efraim, the better blessing. As it says in the Torah, "And Yisrael placed his right hand on Efraim and he is the younger one, and his left on Menashe..."

But the interesting thing here is that Menashe never seems to be jealous of Efraim. Indeed, they are close and loving, as brothers should be.

What is the difference between Yosef and his brothers and Efraim and Menashe? Why doesn't Menashe begin a campaign of revenge and hatred against his younger brother, Efraim?

The answer may lie in the relationship of our forefathers to their children. When Yaacov showed favoritism to Yosef, the brothers automatically assumed that Yosef was to be the chosen one, the brother who would succeed their father. This seemed reasonable, since Avraham and Yitzhak had chosen only one child as their successor, while all other children were ignored. For Yosef's brothers, history was repeating itself.

They never asked their father why he felt so strongly about Yosef. They never thought that they could have a place in Jewish history as well.

But Yosef, remembering what happened with his brothers, immediately asks his father to explain his actions. Yaacov tells him that both brothers will rise to greatness, but that Efraim's descendants will be greater than Menashe's, so Efraim is to receive the greater blessing.

Menashe accepts this. Had the brothers asked their father to explain his actions, they might have understood that they too bore the seeds of greatness.

We must learn an important lesson here. Assuming you know what is behind another person's actions is often not enough. If a situation is unclear, you must seek to clarify it. Communication is the key to a successful relationship, whether between father and son, husband and wife, or just between friends.

THE HAFTARAH CONNECTION

(Kings I 2:1)

In our Parsha, Yaacov, the third and final patriarch, gathers his children around him before he dies. Yaacov gives them their blessings, and imparts his wisdom and his final request.

Our Haftarah deals with very much the same issue. King David is nearing the end of his days. He's already decided that Solomon will be his successor. Before he passes on to the next world, he calls his son to his side and tells him to continue in God's path. He then asks Solomon to fulfill his last requests.

 **TELL IT WITH A SMILE** The Sages of Chelm saw a blessing in everything.

A fire broke out one night in the city of Chelm, and all the inhabitants quickly rushed to put it out. When the fire was extinguished, the Rabbi got up and spoke to the citizens: "My friends, this fire was a miracle sent from heaven."

Everyone in the crowd was surprised, and the Rabbi quickly explained.

"Look at it this way," he said. "If it weren't for the bright flames, how would we have been able to see how to put the fire out on such a dark night?"

THE BOOK OF
SHEMOT

THIS WEEK IN THE PARSHA

A simple, straightforward exposition
of the weekly reading.

TABLE TALK
DVAR TORAH

A brief, cogent talk about the
weekly reading that can be
repeated at the Shabbat table.

FOOD
FOR
THOUGHT

Questions and concepts for
you to think about.

GEMMATRIA

Discusses the numerical value
of words found in the Parsha.

WISDOM
OF THE
SAGES

Rabbinic pearls of wisdom.

THE HAFTARAH CONNECTION

Explains how the Haftarah
connects to the weekly Parsha.

TELL IT WITH A
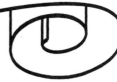
SMILE

A short humorous anecdote
that relates to the Parsha.

שמות

THIS WEEK IN THE PARSHA

A New Pharaoh Arises in Egypt

Yaacov brought his family, 70 people in all, down to Egypt. But a generation later B'nai Yisrael (the Jewish people) have become so numerous that they fill the land.

A new Pharaoh takes over the throne of Egypt. Fearing that B'nai Yisrael may one day join the enemies of Egypt and help conquer the land from within, Pharaoh enslaves the Jewish people and uses them to build the cities of Pitom and Ramses. Yet, the more Pharaoh oppresses them, the more the Jewish people multiply.

Pharaoh's Decree

Pharaoh tells the Jewish midwives, Shifra and Puah, to kill all the male Jewish babies that they deliver. The midwives fear God and disobey Pharaoh. When Pharaoh demands to know why they did not obey him, they explain that the Jewish women give birth before they arrive. For saving Jewish lives, God rewards the midwives with large families.

When Pharaoh sees that his plan hasn't worked, he commands all his people, saying, "Every boy who is born must be thrown in the Nile River, but every girl will be allowed to live."

Moshe is Born

A man of the House of Levi marries Levi's daughter. She gives birth to a boy and hides him for three months. When she can't hide him any longer, she builds a small ark and puts him inside. She places the ark in the reeds along the river bank of the Nile, where his sister keeps watch.

Pharaoh's daughter comes to bathe by the river. When she sees the ark, she sends one of her slaves to retrieve it. When she opens the ark and sees the baby, she knows he is a Jew.

The baby's sister offers to bring someone to nurse the baby. She brings the infant's mother, who is paid by Pharaoh's daughter, to take care of the baby until he grows up.

When the baby is older, his mother brings him to Pharaoh's daughter. She adopts him, and calls him **Moshe**, which means, "I *drew* him out of the water."

Moshe is Forced to Flee Egypt

One day Moshe goes out among the Jewish people. He sees an Egyptian beating a Jew. Looking around to make sure no one is watching, he then kills the Egyptian, burying him in the sand.

The next day Moshe goes out again. When he sees a Jew lifting his hand to hit another Jew, Moshe rebukes him for hitting his brother. The Jew replies, "Who made you officer and judge? Are you going to kill me like you killed the Egyptian?"

Moshe realizes his deed has become known and, fearing Pharaoh will kill him, flees to Midyan.

In Midyan, Moshe encounters some shepherds harassing the daughters of the priest of Midyan, and comes to their aid. When they repeat the story to their father, Reuel, he tells them to bring Moshe to their home. Moshe marries Reuel's daughter, Tzipporah. She gives birth to a son, and Moshe names him **Gershom**, which means "I have been a *foreigner* in a strange land."

The Burning Bush

The Pharaoh dies and B'nai Yisrael cry to God for help.

God hears their pleas. Remembering His covenant with Avraham, Yitzhak, and Yaacov, he decides to act.

Meanwhile, Moshe is tending his father-in-law's sheep in the area of Mount Horev. An angel of God appears to Moshe in a burning bush. Moshe wonders why the bush is not consumed by the flames.

God calls to Moshe, commanding him to remove his shoes, for he is standing in a holy place. Moshe learns that God has chosen him to liberate the Jewish people from the Egyptians. But he argues that he is unworthy of such a task. God assures Moshe that He will be with him. Moshe is to bring the Jewish people to this mountain so they can serve God.

Moshe says that the Jewish people will want to know the name of God. What should he say? God says to tell them, "I will be Who I will be." Moshe is also to say that the God of their forefathers has sent him.

God tells Moshe to gather the elders of Israel and go to Pharaoh. Moshe is to tell Pharaoh that the Jewish people must leave for three days to sacrifice to God. Pharaoh will not agree and then God will bring plagues on the Egyptians. Ultimately, the Egyptians will be so anxious to have the Jewish people leave their land, they will give them all their wealth.

God Gives Moshe Signs

Moshe insists that the Jewish people will still not believe him. So, God shows Moshe signs that will help him prove that he is God's messenger.

1. Moshe throws his staff on the ground and it turns into a snake. When he picks it up by its tail, it turns back into a staff.

2. Moshe puts his hand inside his robe. When he takes it out, it is leprous, white as snow. When he puts it back inside, it returns to normal.

If the people still do not believe him, then he is to use a third sign:

3. Moshe is to take water from the river and throw it on the ground. When it hits the ground, it will turn into blood.

Moshe continues to refuse God's mission for him, claiming that he has a speech impediment. God tells Moshe that since He gives people the ability to speak, He will make sure Moshe has no trouble speaking. But Moshe still feels unworthy of the mission. God becomes angry and relents, telling Moshe that his brother, Aaron, will speak for him.

Tzipporah Saves Moshe

Moshe returns to his father-in-law, Reuel, who is also called Yitro, packs up his family, and leaves. On the way to Egypt they stop at an inn, where God confronts Moshe for not circumcising his son. Tzipporah saves Moshe by circumcising their son.

Moshe and Aaron Stand Before Pharaoh

Aaron meets Moshe in the desert and they go to Egypt. There, they deliver God's message to the Jewish people. Seeing the signs, the people believe them.

Moshe and Aaron go to Pharaoh and tell him that the Jewish people must leave in order to sacrifice to God. Pharaoh says, "Who is God that I should listen to Him and let you go?"

Pharaoh accuses Moshe and Aaron of looking for excuses to create holidays for the Jewish people. He tells the taskmasters to stop giving B'nai Yisrael straw with which to make bricks. But the Jewish people must still continue to make the same number of bricks that they made when they had straw.

The foremen of the Jewish people are made to suffer. They confront Moshe and Aaron and blame them for these new hardships. When Moshe complains to God, he is told not to worry. Moshe will soon see how God will take the Jewish people out of Pharaoh's land.

WISDOM OF THE SAGES
"Remove your shoes from your feet." (3:5)

The correct path is always full of thorns and rocks. When you wear shoes, you don't feel them. Walk barefoot, however, and you become sensitive to the smallest thorn or pebble. That was the point God was trying to get across to Moshe.

God told Moshe, who was just about to become the leader of the Jewish people, to take off his shoes. The leader of a nation must be sensitive to every emotion, every problem that his people experience.

"Slow of speech, and slow of tongue am I." (4:10)

How did Moshe get his speech impediment?

The Midrash tells us that when Moshe was a child, sitting on Pharaoh's lap, he suddenly reached for the king's crown. Pharaoh's advisors told him to kill Moshe because this was a clear sign that the child would try to dethrone him. Pharaoh didn't want to kill Moshe, but what if the advisors were correct?

One of the advisors suggested that Pharaoh place sparkling jewels on one side of the child and hot coals on the other. If the child touched the jewels, then he would be killed. If he touched the coals, then clearly there was nothing to be afraid of. Moshe reached for the jewels, but at the last minute the angel Gavriel moved his hand to the hot coals. The coals burned his fingers and, putting his hand in his mouth, Moshe burned his tongue and lips. From then on he spoke with a speech impediment.

THE HAFTARAH CONNECTION

(Yeshayahu 27:6)

From the 70 people who originally came down to Egypt, a whole nation developed. The reason they survived and prospered is that, although they were in exile, they were strong and unbending.

In the Haftarah, the prophet Yeshayahu compares the Jewish nation in exile to the roots of a tree. He tells the people that the tree can't survive without roots. Even though we can't see the roots, they are there and give life to the tree. As long as the people maintain their Jewish roots, even in the depths of exile, God will support them.

TABLE TALK
DVAR TORAH

When Moshe went to tell the Jews about their imminent redemption, he didn't go empty-handed. God gave him three signs to make certain that B'nai Yisrael would listen to him.

First, Moshe was told to throw his staff on the ground. The staff then became a snake. When Moshe picked it up, it turned back to a staff.

Second, Moshe was told to put his hand inside his robe. His hand became leprous. He then put his hand back inside his robe and it returned to normal.

Third, Moshe was told to take water from the Nile and throw it onto the ground. Upon touching the ground, the water would turn into blood.

There is a very obvious difference between the first two signs and the third sign. In the first two, everything returned to normal. However, in the third, the blood remained. Why?

Our Sages tell us that the first two signs represent the power of the Egyptians.

The staff of Moshe was harmless until God turned it into a snake. The Egyptians might have been as dangerous as vipers, their swords and armor mighty; but just as God turned the snake back into a staff, so too, God would turn the armaments of the Egyptians into putty.

Moshe's hand represented the Egyptians themselves. Moshe showed the people that God has the ability to make the hand sick and also to cure it. So too, God can take the strong hand of the Egyptians and make it weak and sickly.

The third sign was different — it showed the Jewish people something about the land of Egypt. God wanted to demonstrate that Egypt was not a good land and that the Nile River was not necessarily a blessing for the land. This is an important point because, as we will learn, many of the Jews thought that they were leaving Egypt so that God could kill the Egyptians and then bring the Jewish people back to Egypt. They thought that Egypt was the "land of milk and honey."

God showed them that the Nile River could be both a blessing and a curse. And just as the blood did not turn back into water, so too, the Jewish people would never return to Egypt. The Exodus from Egypt would bring the Jewish people to only one land, the land of Israel.

1. Moshe was the greatest leader we ever had, but before becoming the leader of the Jewish people, he was a shepherd. Other Jewish leaders were also shepherds. What is the connection between being a shepherd and being a leader?

2. When Moshe was told to take B'nai Yisrael out of Egypt, he started arguing with God. How could Moshe doubt God's infinite wisdom in sending him?

3. When Pharaoh wanted to punish B'nai Yisrael, he decreed that the taskmasters stop providing straw for the Jewish slaves. Why didn't Pharaoh just raise the quota of bricks that they needed to produce?

GEMMATRIA How long did it take for Pharaoh to realize that God was in charge of the world? Moshe told Pharaoh that God had revealed Himself to the Jewish people, but that Pharaoh would also witness God's power. The Hebrew word for "revealed" is *nikrah*, which has a numeric value of 355.

The Hebrew word *shana* means "year," and has the same numeric value, 355. The ten plagues took a year, which is how long it took for Pharaoh to realize the power of God.

TELL IT WITH A SMILE

Late one night, a burglar broke into a house he thought was empty. He tiptoed through the living room, but suddenly he froze in his tracks when he heard a loud voice say, "Pharaoh is watching you!"

The burglar stopped. Frantically, he looked around. In a dark corner, he spotted a parrot in a bird cage.

He asked the parrot: "Was that you who said Pharaoh is watching me?"

"Yes," admitted the parrot.

The burglar breathed a sigh of relief.

"What's your name?" he asked the parrot.

"Cleopatra," answered the bird.

"That's an odd name for a parrot," snickered the burglar. "What kind of a person would name a parrot Cleopatra?"

"The same kind of person who named that ferocious German shepherd over there, Pharaoh," squawked the parrot.

וארא

THIS WEEK IN THE PARSHA

God Promises Deliverance from Exile

God explains to Moshe that He is the God of his forefathers. He has heard the cries of the Jewish people. God tells Moshe to say to the people that He will bring them out of the Egyptian oppression, deliver them from slavery, redeem them with an outstretched hand, and take them for His people. He will also bring them to the land of Israel.

But the people are so oppressed they will not listen to Moshe.

Who is Moshe?

Amram married Yoheved. Their male children are Aaron and Moshe. Aaron marries Elishevah; they have four sons: Nadav, Avihu, Elazar, and Itamar. Elazar marries and has a son, Pinhas.

Moshe is 80 years old and Aaron is 83 when they first speak to Pharaoh.

Pharaoh's Magicians Fail

When Moshe and Aaron approach Pharaoh, he asks for proof of God's power. Aaron turns his staff into a snake. Pharaoh summons his magicians, and they also turn their staffs into snakes. Aaron's staff then swallows up the Egyptians' staffs. Pharaoh hardens his heart and refuses to admit defeat.

The Plagues

God sends plagues to punish the Egyptians for refusing to let the Jewish people leave Egypt:

Blood — Aaron extends his staff over the Nile River, and the waters turns into blood. Although Pharaoh's magicians are able to duplicate this feat, they cannot turn the blood back into water. Pharaoh doesn't let B'nai Yisrael go.

The waters return to normal after seven days.

Frogs — Aaron points his staff at the lakes and rivers, and frogs emerge, covering the land of Egypt. Pharaoh's magicians are able to do this too. Pharaoh summons Moshe and Aaron and tells them he will let the Jewish people go if they pray to their God to stop the plague.

Moshe prays, and all the frogs die. But again, Pharaoh hardens his heart and refuses to let the Jewish people go.

Lice — Aaron strikes the sand with his staff, and the sand in all of Egypt turns into lice.

The magicians can't duplicate this feat, but Pharaoh still remains obstinate.

Wild Beasts — God sends wild beasts to attack the Egyptians. However, no beasts enter the Goshen area, where the Jewish people live.

At this point, Pharaoh summons Moshe and Aaron and agrees to let them sacrifice to their God, but only if they do so inside Egypt. Moshe tells Pharaoh that they must leave Egypt because the animals they sacrifice are sacred to the Egyptians, and may provoke the Egyptians to attack the Jews. Pharaoh agrees on condition that Moshe pray to God to stop the plague.

When the plague is over, Pharaoh hardens his heart again.

Animal Disease — The Egyptians' livestock remaining in the fields die of disease. Even though Pharaoh discovers that the plague hasn't affected the livestock of the Jewish people, he remains obstinate.

Boils — Moshe and Aaron take a handful of furnace soot and throw it into the air. The soot causes a rash, which turns into boils on man and beast. God hardens Pharaoh's heart, and he won't let the Jewish people leave.

Hail — Moshe points his staff at the sky and a heavy hailstorm mixed with fire descends upon Egypt. Only in Goshen is the sky clear.

Pharaoh admits to Moshe and Aaron that he has sinned. God is just, he cries, and he and the Egyptians are wrong. He begs Moshe and Aaron to pray for him. Moshe agrees, even though he is aware that Pharaoh doesn't fear God.

As God had predicted, Pharaoh hardens his heart as soon as the plague is over.

1. **When the Torah mentions Moshe and Aaron together, sometimes Moshe is mentioned first, and sometimes Aaron is mentioned first. Why?**

2. **Why does the Torah tell us how old Moshe and Aaron were at the time they spoke to Pharaoh? What relevance does it have to what they were about to do?**

3. **Every third plague descended on Pharaoh and the Egyptians without a warning. Why?**

WISDOM OF THE SAGES

"And these are the heads of their houses." (6:14)

Rashi explains that the reason the genealogy of the tribes is written is to show us that Moshe and Aaron came from the tribe of Levi.

Why is it so important that we know which tribe Moshe was from?

When people have high regard for someone, they tend to idolize them. Moshe is going to become the greatest leader in the history of the Jewish nation. God wants to make sure that we will always remember that Moshe was just a flesh-and-blood individual who came from flesh-and-blood parents.

"And I will harden Pharaoh's heart." (7:3)

How could God take away Pharaoh's free choice?

There are two ways to rid yourself of a bad habit, such as smoking. One way is to have enough sheer willpower just to stop. The other is to smoke so much that you get sick of it and never want to do it again.

God wanted Pharaoh to behave more righteously. But Pharaoh had no willpower; he only wanted to do evil. So God hardened his heart. He gave Pharaoh a massive dose of evil, which forced him, in the end, to see how evil he had become.

"It is the Finger of God." (8:15)

The plague of lice was the first one in which Pharaoh's magicians conceded that God was greater than they were. Why couldn't the magicians duplicate this plague as they had the first two?

The Egyptian magicians were unable to perform magic on anything less than the size of barley. Only God could create something from a particle this small. Since the dust from which the lice had come was smaller than barley, the Egyptians realized that this plague must have come from God.

 The magicians tell Pharaoh that the plague of lice is the Finger of God, "Etzbah Elokim."

God has many names, but the Hebrew name, *Elokim*, which has the numeric value of 86, signifies God as a judge.

The numeric value of the Hebrew phrase, *Hu dayan,* which means "He is a judge," also adds up to 86.

THE HAFTARAH CONNECTION

(Yehezkel 28:25)

In our Parsha, God promises to free the Jews from slavery and bring them to a better land. God accomplishes this by punishing Pharaoh and the Egyptians.

Our Haftarah follows almost the same pattern, but takes place hundreds of years later, when the Jews are in exile.

God appears to the prophet Yehezkel and tells him that he is going to bring the Jews back to their homeland, where they will once again thrive.

Just like Moshe, Yehezkel is told to warn the Egyptians that God is getting ready to punish them.

TABLE TALK
DVAR TORAH

In our Parsha, God sends Moshe to appear before Pharaoh and convince him that he is God's messenger. God tells Moshe to tell Aaron to transform his staff into a snake. This doesn't convince Pharaoh, because Egypt is famed for its first-class magicians.

Why would turning a staff into a snake convince Pharaoh that Moshe was special?

After all, maybe Moshe and Aaron were like those people who were adept at pulling rabbits out of hats. The fact that the Egyptian sorcerers were able to match their powers seems to suggest that what Moshe and Aaron did was just a magic trick.

But the Midrash lets us in on two very interesting points. First, while Aaron's staff actually turned into a snake, the Egyptians' staffs only took on *the shape* of snakes. Second, when Aaron's staff swallowed the other staffs, it didn't get any bigger! How was such a thing possible?

While Pharaoh was pondering this problem, perhaps he was reminded of something else. The previous ruler of Egypt had also stood face-to-face with one of the Jewish people. That Pharaoh had dreamt of cows and ears of corn. There too, the thin cows ate the fat ones without getting any fatter. The same was true of the seven scrawny stalks of corn when they ate the seven healthy ones. The only one able to interpret the dream was Yosef, a Jewish slave.

Now we see the greatness of God's plan: He wanted to remind Pharaoh who he was dealing with. Sure enough, as soon as Pharaoh sees this miracle, he realizes that Moshe is from the same stock as Yosef, the man who had become second only to the Pharaoh himself.

Each and every one of us comes from that stock.
Pharaohs of the world, beware!

 **TELL IT WITH A SMILE**

Max walked into the classroom a half hour late.

"Why are you so late?" asked the teacher.

"My father needed me at home," replied Max.

"Couldn't your father have used someone else instead of you?" asked the teacher angrily.

"No," answered Max. "I had to be punished."

בא

THIS WEEK IN THE PARSHA

The Plagues Continue

Locusts — Moshe tells Pharaoh that the next plague will be swarming locusts. Pharaoh's servants appeal to the king to let the Jewish people go. Moshe says he wants to take everyone, even the cattle and sheep, to hold a festival in honor of God. Pharaoh insists that Moshe leave with only the Jewish men, and then expels Moshe and Aaron from the palace.

Moshe extends his hand over the land of Egypt and God sends an east wind, which drives the locusts into Egypt. There was never a plague of locusts like this before, nor would there ever be again.

Pharaoh admits that he has committed a crime against God and asks Moshe and Aaron to pray to God to remove the plague.

God removes the locusts and hardens Pharaoh's heart so that he won't let the Jewish people leave Egypt.

Darkness — Moshe stretches his hand toward heaven and an all-enveloping darkness covers the land of Egypt for three days. It is so severe that people can't see one another. However, wherever the Jewish people live, there is light.

Pharaoh tells Moshe to take everyone and leave, but they must leave their cattle behind. Moshe informs Pharaoh that not only will they take their own cattle, but Pharaoh himself will provide them with cattle. Incensed, Pharaoh tells him that the next time Moshe sees the king's face, he will die.

Introducing the Tenth Plague

God tells Moshe that He will bring one more plague on Egypt, and then Pharaoh will let them leave. The Jews are to ask for gold and silver vessels from the Egyptians. They will leave as a wealthy nation.

Moshe warns Pharaoh that, at about midnight, God is going to kill every firstborn Egyptian, including the firstborn animals. After that, Pharaoh's servants will beg him to let the Jewish people leave Egypt.

The Pesah Sacrifice

God tells Moshe and Aaron that the month of Nissan is to be the first month of the year.

Every Jewish family is to take a lamb on the tenth day of the month. The lamb is to be sacrificed on the afternoon of the fourteenth day. The lamb is to be roasted, then eaten during the ensuing night, with *matzah* and *maror,* and in great haste. The blood from the sacrifice is to be placed on the two doorposts and on the beam above the door of each house. The blood on the doorposts will serve as a reminder to God that He should pass over that house on His way to destroying the firstborn in Egypt.

The Jewish people are to eat matzah for seven days, from the fifteenth through the twenty-first of Nissan. Before eating the matzah, they are to clean their houses of all leaven.

When they arrive in the Holy Land and their children ask them what they are doing on Pesah, they should reply that they are sacrificing to God because He passed over the Jewish houses during the death of the firstborn.

120

The Tenth Plague

Death of the firstborn — At exactly midnight, God kills every firstborn Egyptian, man and animal. Pharaoh goes to Moshe and Aaron and tells them to take their belongings and leave.

The Exodus Begins

The Jewish people are in such a hurry to leave that their dough has no time to rise. The Egyptians are so glad to be rid of them, they give the Jews their gold and silver.

About 600,000 men over the age of 20 leave Egypt, along with their families.

God tells Moshe that the Exodus is to be remembered in the Spring, on the same day every year. The Jewish people are to tell their children that they were taken out of Egypt, because B'nai Yisrael sacrificed the lamb to God.

The words in the Torah dealing with the Exodus are to be placed as a sign on their arms and a reminder on their heads. (The words are enclosed in tefillin.)

Commemorating the Exodus

God gives Moshe and Aaron laws relating to Pesah. The lamb is to be eaten in groups; no stranger or uncircumcised male may eat from the sacrifice.

Furthermore, when the Jews arrive in Israel, they must give their firstborn males — humans and animals — to God. The humans will be redeemed with money, the non-kosher animals with a lamb.

When their children ask them to explain this practice, they are to say that God killed all the firstborn in Egypt, except the firstborn of the Jewish people.

WISDOM OF THE SAGES

The Midrash says that the Egyptians could actually feel the plague of darkness. But, in this plague, the Jews also suffered. All those not worthy of leaving Egypt were killed during the darkness. Why now? Because God did not want the Egyptians to witness the death of Jews.

During the plague of darkness, "The Jews had light where they lived." (10:23)

Every Jewish soul has a spark of light. However, what happens to that spark is dependent on "where they live." Because our environment can change us, our light can be hidden by the darkness around us. But the light is always there. That is why one must not give up on a fellow Jew. The light of his soul is always there, even though it may be hard to see.

"This month shall be for you the first month of the year." (12:2)

Why is this the first commandment given to the people?

Part of what makes a person a slave is that time isn't his own. God wanted to show the Jewish nation that even though they now serve Him, they have control over time. *They* will decide how long a month and year are going to be.

In the land of Israel, the Sanhedrin, the ruling court of the Jewish nation, decided when the month begins and ends, based on when the moon was seen.

"These words must also be a sign on your arm and a reminder in between your eyes." (13:9)

From this verse we learn some of the laws of tefillin. One box goes on the upper arm, the other on the head, in that order. Why is this order so important?

The tefillin of the hand is placed near the heart, while the tefillin of the head goes between the eyes. A person sins with his eyes and his heart. However, the heart is considered a greater source of sinning than the eyes, so we try to subdue it by first placing the tefillin on the arm near the heart.

1. The lamb that B'nai Yisrael had to slaughter for Pesah could only be eaten roasted. Why not in other ways as well?

2. Based on our Parsha, a person is supposed to eat matzah for seven days. However, in Devarim 16:8, there seems to be a different number of days. How can you explain the difference?

3. God told us to consecrate the firstborn because they belong to Him. Why only the firstborn? After all, don't we all belong to God?

TELL IT WITH A SMILE

When Chaim went into the hospital for an operation, he brought his siddur, tallit, and tefillin with him.

The following morning, he rose early and started putting on his tefillin. The patient in the adjoining bed looked at him with amazement, and exclaimed, "No wonder people say the Jews are brilliant! You haven't been in the hospital 24 hours and you're already taking your own blood pressure!"

TABLE TALK
DVAR TORAH

In our Parsha, we read, "And Moshe said to the nation, Remember this day that you left Egypt, the place of bondage, for God took you out with a strong hand. (Therefore) you shall not eat *hametz*." (13:3)

The obligation to recall the Exodus is stressed in many places in the Torah. We are required once a year at the Pesah seder to recount in detail the story of the redemption. But we make mention of it every day in our prayers.

What is the reason that so much emphasis is placed on an event that occurred so long ago? Why, in the first commandment, does God identify Himself as the One Who took us out of Egypt, and not, for example, as the One Who created the world? And why are so many mitzvot (e.g., Shabbat, tefillin, Sukkot, etc.) connected with the Exodus?

It seems clear that historical fact is not the issue here. There is a deeper, underlying reason that we "must see ourselves as if we left Egypt." Why?

In order to answer these questions, we must pose one last problem. Why did God take the Jews out of Egypt in such a spectacular fashion? Was it really necessary to bring ten plagues, when God could have just as easily "unhardened" Pharaoh's heart?

The Ramban explains that the main purpose of the plagues was not to punish the Egyptians, but rather to educate both them and us. There were many Egyptians who doubted God's existence, His supreme rule, and His involvement in the world. No one, however, could witness the miracles that transpired, one after another, and still retain his atheism or belief in idols. The plagues illustrated, beyond a shadow of a doubt, that God is all-powerful. They showed that God *does* take an active role in the world, and that He is concerned with the actions of man.

The message was so strong that even Pharaoh, who completely denied God's existence, was forced to exclaim: "God will rule forever!"

However, it wasn't only the Egyptians who had forgotten about God. The Jews, too, were in need of re-education, assimilated as they were into Egyptian culture. B'nai Yisrael had to experience God firsthand.

No individual witnessed the creation of the world. But millions experienced the Exodus and told the story to subsequent generations. If God sent the plague of blood, it must be God Who gives us water. If God slew the firstborn, it must be God Who gives us life. And so, for B'nai Yisrael, the Exodus from Egypt has become *the* national experience; it is the turning point of our existence as a nation, and part of each Jew's heritage.

THE HAFTARAH CONNECTION

(Yermeyahu 46:13)

Our Parsha continues with the final plagues of destruction sent by God to the Egyptians.

This Haftarah, like the previous one, deals with the destruction of Egypt.

God tells Yermeyahu to tell the King of Bavel to attack Egypt. God will see to it that the Egyptians are destroyed, just as He once destroyed them with the plagues.

The prophet tells the Jewish people that God will make sure that they survive, just as He made sure B'nai Yisrael survived the ten plagues.

GEMMATRIA The Hebrew word *bo,* which means "come," has a numeric value of three. It also gives us a hint as to how many plagues will be discussed in the Parsha, three.

God told Moshe to "come" to Pharaoh. The number three represents the three plagues of our Parsha.

בשלח

THIS WEEK IN THE PARSHA

The Splitting of the Red Sea

Before the Jewish people leave Egypt, Moshe takes Yosef's coffin with them, as Yosef had requested.

God uses a roundabout route to take the Jews out of Egypt. He doesn't want the Jewish people to turn back to Egypt if they come under attack by another nation.

There is a pillar of cloud to guide the people by day and a pillar of fire to guide them by night.

The Jewish people camp in a valley between Migdol and the Red Sea. Pharaoh thinks that B'nai Yisrael are trapped and leads his army to attack them.

The Jewish people reach the banks of the sea and complain to Moshe. They want to know why he freed them if they will just be killed in the desert. Slavery is better than death, they say. Moshe assures them that God will fight for them.

God tells Moshe to raise his staff and the water will split. Meanwhile, the angel that was traveling in front of the people, and the pillar of cloud, both move to the rear. They act as a barrier between the Egyptians and the Jewish people.

Moshe raises his staff and the sea splits. B'nai Yisrael cross on dry land. When the Egyptians follow, the sea collapses on them.

The Jewish people are in awe of God as they see the Egyptians' bodies dead on the shore. They truly believe in God, and in His servant, Moshe.

A Song to God

Moshe and B'nai Yisrael sing a song of praise to God. They praise Him for killing the Egyptians in such a miraculous way.

Miriam, Aaron's sister, takes a drum in her hand and sings a song to God as all the women follow her lead.

The Waters of Marah

B'nai Yisrael arrive in Marah, which means "bitter." They complain that the water is bitter and they have nothing to drink. God shows Moshe a special tree, which he throws into the water. The water becomes sweet. In Marah, God gives B'nai Yisrael laws and tests their faithfulness.

God tells Moshe that if B'nai Yisrael will obey His commandments, He will not bring upon them any of the sicknesses that He brought on the Egyptians.

Food from Heaven

On the fifteenth day of the second month after they left Egypt, the Jewish people complain to Moshe and Aaron that they are dying of starvation.

God tells Moshe that He will make bread rain down from the sky, but that each person may only gather what he can eat. God wants to test B'nai Yisrael to see if they will keep His commandments.

That afternoon a flock of quail come and cover the camp. The people catch and eat the quail.

In the morning, a layer of dew covers the ground. When the dew evaporates, something that looks like a white coriander seed and tastes like a honey pancake appears on the ground. B'nai Yisrael call it *mahn,* which in Hebrew means "What is it?"

It can also mean "a portion of food." Moshe tells them to gather one *omer* (about two quarts) per person. When they measure what they have gathered, every person ends up with exactly one omer — no matter how much he thinks he gathered!

Moshe tells B'nai Yisrael not to leave any mahn over for the next day. Some people don't listen to Moshe, and their leftover mahn rots. Moshe is angry with them.

On Friday, the nation is to gather a double portion of mahn, in order to have enough for Shabbat. The mahn gathered on Friday will not spoil. On Shabbat, some men go into the field to gather mahn, but they find nothing.

Moshe has Aaron fill a jug with an omer of mahn as a keepsake for their descendants. B'nai Yisrael eat the mahn during their wanderings, for 40 years.

Moshe Hits the Rock

When B'nai Yisrael arrive in Rephidim, again they complain about a lack of water. Moshe asks God to do something before the people stone him.

God tells Moshe to take his staff and go with the elders of the people to Horev, where God will be waiting by a rock. Moshe is to strike the rock with his staff.

When Moshe hits the rock, water starts to flow from it. Moshe calls the place Masah U'mriva, which means "testing and argument," because the people argued and tested God.

Amalek Attacks

The nation of Amalek attacks B'nai Yisrael at Rephidim. Moshe tells Yehoshua to choose the men who will fight Amalek.

The following day, Moshe, Aaron, and Hur go to the top of a

hill while Yehoshua, Moshe's protege, takes the men into battle. When Moshe raises his hands, B'nai Yisrael begin to defeat Amalek; but when Moshe lowers his hands, Amalek gets stronger. Moshe becomes tired and Aaron and Hur place a rock under him so he can sit down. They each support one of his hands.

In this way, Yehoshua and his men defeat Amalek.

God tells Moshe to write down what has happened with Amalek. God promises that one day He will utterly wipe out the memory of Amalek for what they did.

WISDOM
OF THE
SAGES

"God will fight for you, and you will remain silent." (14:14)

Whenever the Satan badmouths the Jews, there is usually a ready answer for the accusation.

However, one accusation is hard to rebut: that some Jews don't show respect in places of worship, and talk during prayer.

That's why, when the Torah says, "God will fight for you," it means He will fight your battles with the Satan, but you must "remain silent." Don't talk to others during times of prayer.

"And B'nai Yisrael called it mahn." (16:31)

Why did B'nai Yisrael pick this name for the food that fell from heaven?

Mahn in Hebrew is spelled with two letters, *mem* and *nun*. They are the only nasal letters in the Hebrew alphabet. If you hold your nose and try to pronounce these letters, they sound funny, as though you have a nose cold.

Mahn tasted like whatever food a person desired. But the

sense of taste is related directly to the sense of smell. If you can't smell a food, you can't taste it. If the person eating the mahn had a nose cold, then the mahn had no taste. So the people called it by the two nasal letters in the Hebrew alphabet.

"As long as Moshe held his hands up, Israel would be winning, but as soon as he let his hands down, Amalek would win." (17:11)

"Do Moshe's hands decide war?" asks the Mishnah. What's the connection between Moshe's hands and the outcome of the war?

The Mishnah answers that, when Moshe's hands were raised, the Jews would look up to God and He would save them. When Moshe's hands were lowered, the Jews didn't think about God and began to lose the battle.

 When God told Moshe that He was going to wipe out all remembrance of Amalek, He used the Hebrew phrase *maho emheh,* "I will erase." The numeric value of these words comes to 107.

When Haman of the Purim story rose up to destroy the Jewish people, he was bound to fail because he was a descendant of Amalek. The Hebrew words *ze Haman,* which means "this is Haman," also add up to 107.

From this, we see that God was letting the Jews know that He would destroy Haman.

TABLE TALK
DVAR TORAH

The first mitzvah that B'nai Yisrael receive after leaving Egypt is Shabbat. While Shabbat involves many laws, B'nai Yisrael are given only a few specific ones.

Why is it that, of all the commandments that the Jewish nation is destined to receive, Shabbat is the first one given to them upon leaving Egypt?

And why is the particular law of preparing on Friday for Shabbat mentioned? Why not start with the basic prohibition of making a fire?

In order to answer these questions, we must remember that the Israelites have just been released from the most agonizing slavery imaginable. They are being molded into a nation, but still don't know what God expects of them.

It is precisely for this reason that Shabbat was designated as the first mitzvah.

Shabbat is a day of rest, but it is also a time when families get together. It is the break from the workweek, and it is the time when relationships are solidified and revitalized. God wanted to emphasize to this new nation that an important element of nationhood is the passing of traditions from one generation to the next, and what better vehicle to accomplish this than designating a special "heritage" day — Shabbat.

The preparation of food on Friday for Shabbat was chosen as the first specific law about Shabbat because the culinary experience is, for the Jew, a joyous family experience. God wanted to show this budding nation that it is not only *shver tzu zein a yid*, "difficult to be Jew," but also enjoyable. We are commanded to serve God in happiness and good spirit.

It seems that God did not want to begin the laws of Shabbat

with laws of prohibition, but rather, with laws that would bind the Jewish people with a sense of joy and tradition. This helped B'nai Yisrael understand what serving their new master, God, was all about.

1. As soon as B'nai Yisrael saw the Egyptians coming toward them, they became angry at Moshe for taking them out of Egypt. After having just witnessed all the miracles in Egypt, how could they doubt God's ability to protect them?

2. When the Jewish people sang their song to God, the women used musical instruments but the men didn't. Why?

3. God says that he will wipe out all memory of Amalek. What did Amalek do that merited such Divine retribution? They weren't the only nation in history to fight with the Jews, yet they have the distinction of being singled out by God for destruction. Why?

TELL IT WITH A SMILE

Jeremy had been in the navy for three months, but this was his first time setting sail. The ship was in the middle of the ocean when suddenly a great storm blew in.

Jeremy hung onto the rail of the boat for dear life. He asked the sailor next him, "How far are we from land?"

"Only four or five miles," replied the sailor cheerfully.

Jeremy felt relieved, but then remembered that they were three days out at sea. He quickly asked, "In which direction?"

"Straight down," grinned the mate.

THE HAFTARAH CONNECTION

(Shoftim 4:4)

In our Parsha, B'nai Yisrael finally leave Egypt. Pharaoh chases them and God performs one of the greatest miracles of all times by splitting the Red Sea. The Jews pass through safely, but the Egyptians drown when they try to follow. Moshe then leads the nation in a song of praise to God.

In our Haftarah, the Jewish people are being oppressed by King Yavin of Amor and his general, Sisrah. Although B'nai Yisrael are greatly outnumbered, Devorah, a prophetess, rallies the Jews to fight the oppressor. Miraculously, they win.

After the war, Devorah leads the nation in a song of praise to God.

יתרו

THIS WEEK IN THE PARSHA

Yitro Gives Advice to Moshe

When Yitro hears what God has done for the Jewish people, he brings Moshe's wife, Tzipporah, and her two sons to Moshe. When he arrives at the camp of the Jewish people, Yitro praises God and brings sacrifices.

When he sees Moshe judging all the people, Yitro advises him to create a system of judges so that Moshe can deal exclusively with the most difficult legal problems.

Mount Sinai

B'nai Yisrael arrive at Mount Sinai in the third month after the Exodus. Moshe goes up the mountain. God tells him that if the people will obey His commandments, they will become a kingdom of Kohanim and a holy nation. Moshe repeats this message to B'nai Yisrael and they shout, "We will do what God asks!"

Moshe tells the people that God will descend on Mount Sinai in three days. He sets a boundary to make sure the people don't go up the mountain. B'nai Yisrael must purify themselves and immerse their clothing.

On the day the Torah is given, thunder and lightning envelop Mount Sinai. A heavy cloud descends and the mountain is covered with smoke. B'nai Yisrael tremble at all that they see and hear. A loud blast of a ram's horn is heard.

The Ten Commandments

On the tablets that God gives Moshe are written the Ten Commandments:

I am your God.

You shall not have any other gods besides Me.

Do not take God's name in vain.

Remember the Shabbat to keep it holy.

Honor your father and mother.

Do not commit murder.

Do not commit adultery.

Do not steal.

Do not testify falsely.

Do not be envious of your neighbor.

The Fear of God

B'nai Yisrael are so frightened by all they see and hear that they ask Moshe to speak to them, instead of God. They are terrified that if God continues speaking directly to them, they will die. Moshe tries to calm them, but B'nai Yisrael keep their distance while Moshe enters the smoke, where the Divine Presence is waiting.

More Laws on Mount Sinai

God tells Moshe additional laws, including:
1) Do not make gods of silver or gold.

2) **Make an earthen altar upon which you will sacrifice to God.**

3) **Do not build an altar out of cut stone.**

4) **Do not go up the altar by steps; use a ramp, so that your nakedness will not be revealed.**

WISDOM OF THE SAGES

God wanted to give the Torah on a mountain, but it was not clear which mountain should have this honor.

All the mountains assembled before God and explained why the Torah should be given on them. The tall mountains said the Torah should be given on them because of their height. The beautiful ones said their beauty merited their getting the Torah.

There was one mountain, however, Mount Sinai, that felt it did not deserve such an honor. It had no unusual physical characteristics; it was just a plain mountain. But God told the mountains that the Torah would be given on Mount Sinai. The Torah could only be given on a humble mountain.

The same is true for people. A person is a vessel for the Torah. When a man is humble, the vessel is empty, giving the Torah a chance to fill it. A haughty person doesn't leave any room for the Torah.

"So you shall say to the House of Yaacov, and relate it to the Children of Israel." (19:3)

Rashi explains that "the House of Yaacov" refers to the women, and "the Children of Israel" refers to the men.

Why are the women mentioned before the men? Since the mother is with the child during the formative years, she has the task of teaching the child its first words of Torah. To show the importance of this, the women are mentioned first.

"And they stood at the bottom of the mountain." (19:17)

The Talmud Shabbat (88A) explains that the phrase "bottom of the mountain" has a deeper meaning. The Jews actually stood beneath the mountain. God uprooted the mountain and placed it over them. He told them that if they accepted the Torah, everything would be fine; but if they didn't, they would be buried under the mountain.

How could God force the Jewish nation to accept the Torah?

God told the Jewish people that only the Torah could ensure the world's survival. By holding the mountain over them, He was only reminding them that the future of the world rested with them. If they refused to accept the Torah, not only would they die, but the whole world would perish.

THE HAFTARAH CONNECTION

(Yeshayahu 6:1)

In our Parsha, B'nai Yisrael receive the Torah. They become "a kingdom of Kohanim and a holy nation."

In the Haftarah, God makes it clear to the Jewish people that He expects them to be that holy nation.

Yeshayahu sees God sitting on His throne. Then the angels proclaim that God is holy, and the whole world is filled with His holiness. When Yeshayahu sees the pillars of the Temple shake, he realizes that the Jewish people are not living as a holy nation. They have rejected God's Torah.

TABLE TALK
DVAR TORAH

Yitro was surprised by the way his son-in-law, Moshe, judged the people. How could Moshe expect to judge the whole nation? It seemed like a very inefficient way to judge people. So Yitro suggested creating a formal judiciary system that would leave Moshe free to handle the really big cases.

Yitro's plan was to create a hierarchy of judges. Some judges would have jurisdiction over 10 people, others over 50 people, and there would even be some judges with as many as 1,000 people within their jurisdiction.

Moshe didn't argue with his father-in-law. On the contrary, he accepted Yitro's suggestion and changed the judicial system.

But this all seems rather simplistic. Certainly Yitro was not suggesting anything novel. Every nation has a judicial system. How is it that Moshe, the greatest leader the Jewish nation has ever known, didn't figure this system out on his own?

In order to answer this, we have to understand why Moshe was the sole judge, and exactly how he implemented Yitro's suggestion.

Yitro saw the judicial process mainly as a way of solving monetary problems. He felt that disputes over land and wealth were what brought people to the courts. Moshe shouldn't be bothered with small claims. He needed to devote himself to the big monetary claims.

Moshe saw the judicial process differently. To him, it was first and foremost a process of education, in which the people could learn Torah and thus understand where their problems lay. So when Yitro asked Moshe what he was doing, Moshe answered that he judged between man and his neighbor, and that he taught God's law. That was the system Moshe had set up.

The reason Moshe accepted Yitro's suggestion was that he, too, realized that one man could not complete such a task, especially given his role as leader of *all* the people.

But how did Moshe implement Yitro's suggestions?

Yitro set up different levels of judges: "All the minor cases they will judge, and the *major* ones they will bring to you." In other words, the minor financial cases — the small claims — would be handled by the other judges. Moshe would judge the big money cases, cases more fitting for someone of Moshe's stature.

But Moshe made a slight change. The other judges would hear both minor *and* major cases, and bring the *difficult* cases to him.

Moshe knew that a judge should be able to handle a case that is worth one dollar or a million dollars with the same energy and interest. But difficult cases were another matter. The more difficult cases, the ones that needed better understanding of the Torah, had to come to Moshe for final adjudication because, until the people knew *all* the laws of the Torah, he was the best source of Jewish knowledge.

After all, he was called Moshe the Prophet...and Lawgiver.

GEMMATRIA Moshe is told that God will come and bless all those who mention His divine name. God uses the Hebrew word *avoh,* which means, "I will come," to explain what will happen. The numeric value of avoh is 10.

This teaches us that God will come and bless 10 who pray to Him together.

1. B'nai Yisrael accepted the Torah without asking what was written in it. Why didn't they demand to know what they were committing themselves to? Why did they agree so readily?

2. The Ten Commandments are listed later in the fifth book of the Torah, the book of Devarim. Compare our Parsha with Devarim 5:18. What are the differences? What do these differences teach us?

The butcher came to the synagogue looking for the Rabbi. He needed to ask a question about the condition of a cow he intended to slaughter.

The Rabbi's assistant opened the door and asked, "What do you want?"

"I must see the Rabbi," said the butcher.

"The Rabbi is studying right now."

"Studying!" cried the butcher. "Is Chelm so poor it can't afford a Rabbi who has finished school? Can we only afford a mere student?"

מִשְׁפָּטִים

THIS WEEK IN THE PARSHA

B'nai Yisrael Receive Additional Commandments

These are the social laws B'nai Yisrael received from Moshe:

The Hebrew slave and maidservant

A Jewish slave cannot work for his master for more than six years. At the beginning of the seventh year the master must set him free.

If at the end of six years the Jewish slave doesn't want to be set free, his master takes him to court. There, he places the slave by a doorpost and pierces his ear with an awl. The slave can then serve his master until the end of the national 50-year cycle, called the *Yovel* or Jubilee year.

When a man sells his daughter to be a maidservant, her master may marry her, designate her to be his son's wife, or permit her to pay for her freedom.

Kidnapping and murder

Someone who kidnaps or intentionally kills another person, receives a death sentence. However, if the killing is done unintentionally, then the murderer may seek sanctuary in a place that God has set aside for such people.

Harming a parent

Someone who either hits his parents so that they bleed, or curses them, receives a death sentence.

Personal injury

If a man injures another man, but not fatally, he must compensate the injured man for lost wages, and pay his doctor bills.

If two men fight and one of them hits a pregnant woman, resulting in the death of the fetus, the one responsible must pay the woman for her loss. If the woman herself is hurt, then he must pay for her injuries, under the rule of "An eye for an eye."

Canaanite slaves

If a man knocks out his slave's tooth, or blinds him, he must set the slave free.

Damage done by an ox

An ox that kills someone is stoned to death, and its meat cannot be eaten. If, however, the owner of the ox has been warned that his ox is wild and he doesn't take the necessary safety precautions, the owner is also guilty. He can avoid the death sentence by paying his own value as determined in the marketplace, to the family of the victim.

If an ox kills a slave, the owner of the ox must pay 30 shekels.

If an ox kills an ox, the living ox is sold, and the money is split between the two litigants. The money received from the sale of the dead ox is divided between them as well. However, if the ox that gored is known to be wild, and the owner doesn't take the necessary safety requirements, then the owner must pay full damages.

Property damages

If a man digs a hole in a public place and an ox falls into it and dies, the man must pay the value of the ox to its owner.

If someone sets fire to another man's field, he must pay damages.

If a thief steals cattle or sheep, and they are found unharmed, he must pay double their value. If the thief has slaughtered and sold the animal, he must pay back five times the number of cattle he stole and four times the number of sheep.

If the owner of property feels threatened by a thief and kills the thief, he is not punished.

The watchmen

An unpaid watchman is not held liable for the loss of the object he was watching, as long as he swears that he was not negligent.

A paid watchman is held responsible if the object he was watching is stolen or lost, and he must reimburse the owner. However, if the object breaks, or the animal he was watching dies, he does not have to pay the owner as long as he swears that he could not have prevented what happened.

Someone who borrows an object is responsible to take care of it. He is liable for anything that happens to it, unless the owner is present at the time that something happened to it.

Seduction

If a man seduces a single woman, he must marry her. If her father doesn't agree to the marriage, the seducer must give him 50 shekels.

Occult practices

A witch, or someone who sacrifices to an idol, must be killed.

Oppressing the defenseless

It is forbidden to oppress a stranger in the land because you must remember that once you were strangers in Egypt. It is forbidden to oppress a widow or an orphan because God has special concern for them and will hear their cries.

Money lending

It is prohibited to charge interest to another Jew.

Accepting authority
It is prohibited to curse a judge or king.

Giving God His due
Firstborn children and animals belong to God and must be redeemed in their proper time. All the first fruit must also be brought to God.

Trefe
It is forbidden to eat a dead animal found in the field; such meat should be fed to the dogs.

Courts
Judges must not accept a false report, nor favor a poor man's cause. They must also refrain from taking a bribe, and from killing innocent people.

It is prohibited to follow the multitude in anything evil, or to be a false witness. Keep away from falsehood.

Helping someone with his animals
If a man finds a stray animal, he must return it to the rightful owner.

If an animal is carrying a burden, you must help the owner unload the burden.

If you see your enemy's donkey collapsing under the weight of its load, you must help your enemy to lighten the load.

Special times
For six years the land is to be plowed, but during the seventh year — the Shemmitah year — the land is to rest.

The first six days of the week are set aside to do all the work, and the seventh day is a day of rest.

All three festivals — Sukkot, Pesah, Shavuot — must be kept. During the festivals, there is an obligation to bring a sacrifice to God.

Do not cook a baby goat in its mother's milk
This is the prohibition of eating milk and meat together.

An angel will lead the Jewish people
God tells Moshe that He is going to send an angel to bring B'nai Yisrael to the Promised Land. They must obey the angel and not anger him because he won't forgive their disobedience.

Upon entering the land, the people are not to bow down to idols or follow the ways of the other nations.

If the people obey God's commands, His guiding angel will destroy their enemies.

The Land of Israel
God tells the people that in the land of Israel, women will not suffer from stillbirths and everyone will live a full life.

God promises to send deadly wasps to drive out the inhabitants of the land.

The Jews are not to make a treaty with the inhabitants of the land.

"We Will Do All That God Has Said!"

Moshe writes down all of God's words. In the morning, he builds an altar at the base of Mount Sinai, and erects twelve pillars representing the twelve tribes. He sends some men to bring offerings to God.

Moshe reads the Book of the Covenant to the people. They reply, "We will do all that God has said!"

Moshe goes up the mountain, which is covered by a cloud. God calls to Moshe after seven days and tells him to enter the cloud.

Moshe remains on the mountain for 40 days and 40 nights.

WISDOM OF THE SAGES

"And his master shall pierce his ear with an awl." (21:6)

If the slave decides to continue working after six years of slavery, his ear must be pierced. Rashi explains that the ear is chosen because the Jewish people heard God say at Mount Sinai, "B'nai Yisrael are slaves to me!" When someone decides to serve a human being rather than God, he has, in effect, pierced the words of God; therefore, his ear is pierced.

"And he shall cure him." (21:19)

From this verse we learn that a doctor has the right to heal a sick person. God may be the one to do the actual healing, but the doctor is His messenger.

"If a person steals..." (21:37)

Rabbi Bunim from Pshischa said that there are three traits of a thief that will help all of us serve God better.

A thief works at night, in the rain and snow; so must we.

A thief will never give up until he succeeds; so must we.

A thief will steal something, even if he does not know its value; so must we perform the commandments even if we don't know their absolute value.

When the Torah uses the phrase *umkalell aviv*, which means, "and he who curses his father," we are told that this act is punishable by death! The numeric value of umkalell aviv is 225.

The numeric value of the words *zehu b'skelah*, "this one is stoned," has the same value of 225. This is a hint that a person who curses his father is stoned.

147

TABLE TALK
DVAR TORAH

The first law given in our Parsha is about a Jewish slave. If slavery is so bad, how does the Torah allow someone to be sold into slavery?

The general rule of slavery was that a person could be sold only if he stole something and had no money to repay the debt.

If we were to ask anyone today what to do with such a person, the answer would be, "send him to jail." After all, if someone steals — whether he can repay or not — he must be punished. That is how we correct a criminal.

But what happens to the thief in jail?

Once in jail, he is forced to associate with the real thugs — rapists, murderers, etc. He may come into the penal system as a thief, but he has a very good chance of leaving with criminal connections and a criminal education that will lead him to a further life of crime.

Jewish law, however, is not only concerned about the crime, but also the person. The court does not send him to some jail and forget about him; it sends him to another person's house to work off his debt. The court puts him in a place where he can learn good values and emerge a better Jew. Since everyone is influenced by his surroundings, the idea is to create a positive environment instead of a negative one.

In *Ethics of the Fathers* (1:7) it is written, "Nitay the Arbelite says: Keep far away from an evil neighbor, do not associate with the wicked, and do not abandon belief in retribution."

Nitay knew that just from associating with bad people, something rubs off. That is why the tractate Sukkah (56b) states: "Woe to the wicked, woe to his neighbor."

The aim of the Jewish judicial system is to integrate the offender, not alienate him. The Jewish judges were anxious to make sure that the criminal entered society, not after he had paid his debt, but *while* he was paying his debt. In that way the criminal could feel he was accomplishing something in his life, rather than languishing in some jail. And the laws detailing how the master should treat the servant — with respect — help to soften the blow of servitude and turn the thief from a criminal into a productive human being.

THE HAFTARAH CONNECTION

(Yermeyahu 34:8)

The first law given in the Parsha is about purchasing a Jewish slave. The Torah emphasizes that a Jew must be released after six years.

In our Haftarah, Tzidkeyahu, the king of Yehuda, tells the nation to free all their slaves. The decree is given right after an enemy withdraws, and all the Jews have a renewed sense of freedom. But the owners of the slaves soon forcibly take back their slaves.

God tells the prophet Yermeyahu that only He can be master of the Jewish people. God protects His servants. But now that the nation has taken slaves again, God will stop protecting them.

1. We know that honoring one's parents is very important. However, it seems a bit drastic to kill someone for cursing his parents. What is the reason for this severe punishment?

2. Why is it that in the Talmud the phrase "an eye for an eye" is not taken literally?

3. The general penalty for theft is that the thief must pay double. However, if a man steals a sheep and has disposed of it, he has to pay the owner four times. If he steals an ox and has disposed of it, he has to pay the owner five times. What makes sheep and oxen different from other cases of theft? Why is there a difference between a sheep and an ox?

The famous judge from Chelm, Shofet, insisted that justice be done, no matter what the consequences.

One day the ritual slaughterer in the town was caught red-handed stealing some money.

At his trial, the townspeople all showed up. If the ritual slaughterer were found guilty and sent to jail, the people would have no more meat to eat.

Judge Shofet could see that the people were in no mood for justice, so he declared, "It is true that our ritual slaughterer is too valuable to our community to be sent to jail. But justice must be done. And, since we have two shoemakers in town, and we only need one, I decree that one of the shoemakers will be sent to jail instead!"

Donations for the Mishkan

B'nai Yisrael are to build a special sanctuary, called a *Mishkan*, for God. The people are to donate all the materials for the Mishkan.

The Vessels of the Mishkan

God tells Moshe what vessels to build, and what size to make them.

The *Aron* is to be two and one-half cubits long, one and one-half cubits wide, and one and one-half cubits high. (One cubit is approximately two feet.) It is to be made of wood, and covered with a layer of gold on the inside and outside. A band of gold is to surround the Aron.

Two Cherubs, called *K'ruvim*, are to be hammered from the same piece of gold that covers the Aron. They are to face each other with their wings outstretched. They are to be placed on top of the Aron.

God will speak to Moshe from between the two K'ruvim.

The *Shulhan* is to be a special table made of wood, two cubits long, one cubit wide, and one and one-half cubits high. It is to be covered with a layer of gold.

Twelve breads called *Lehem Hapanim* are to be placed on the Shulhan at all times.

The *Menorah* is to be a candelabrum made of pure gold. It is to have six branches extending from a seventh, main branch.

God shows Moshe what a finished Menorah should look like.

The Mishkan is to be surrounded by ten large tapestries that are sewn together and attached to wooden beams, called *K'rashim*, using hooks. To keep the K'rashim in place, Moshe is to make a base for them out of silver.

The *Parohet* is to be a partition made of cloth. Its purpose is to divide the Mishkan between the *Kodesh* — the Holy — and the *Kodesh Hakodashim* — the Holy of Holies.

The Altar, called the *Mizbayah,* is to be hollow and made of wood. Its dimensions are to be five cubits in length by five in width by three cubits in height. Vessels are to be made to remove the ashes that accumulate when the sacrifices are burned, and to perform other functions.

The *Hatzer* is to be an enclosure for the Mishkan. It is to be enclosed by finely woven, twined linen, 100 cubits long and 50 cubits wide. The support pillars are to have bases made of copper.

All the equipment used to make the Mishkan must be made of copper.

WISDOM
OF THE
SAGES
"Speak to B'nai Yisrael and have them take for Me a contribution." (25:2)

Why did God say, "take for Me a contribution"? Shouldn't He have said, "give to Me a contribution"?

It would seem that when the people contributed to the Mishkan, God was giving them something in return. They were giving and also taking.

From this we learn an important lesson in giving charity. When you give to the poor, you actually receive something from God in return. The person who gives charity also takes something at the same time.

"They shall make Me a sanctuary, and I will dwell among them." (25:8)

Why does it say "dwell among them"? Wouldn't "dwell in it" be more accurate? After all, there is only one Mishkan.

Perhaps we are to learn that the Mishkan lies in every Jewish heart. We have to make our heart into a sanctuary fit for God. In this way, we will have the ability to connect to God within our own heart.

"Cover it with pure gold from the inside and outside." (25:11)

The Aron, into which the tablets of the Ten Commandments were placed, had to be covered both on the inside and the outside with pure gold. From this, we learn that a true Torah scholar has to be just as pure on the inside as he portrays himself to be on the outside.

1. The Aron was carried by placing a pole on either side of it. These poles were held in place by rings. The Torah says that, once inserted, the poles were not to be removed from these rings. Why?

2. Why does the Menorah have to be made out of one piece of gold? Why not make the different pieces separately and then attach them?

3. The vessels of the Mishkan had to be practical as well as beautiful. The Mizbayah was large and magnificent, and yet easily portable because it was hollow. How is this principle applied to other vessels in the Mishkan as well?

TABLE TALK
DVAR TORAH

The items in the Mishkan are described in great detail. Three of them — the Aron, the Shulhan, and the Mizbayah — have a golden rim around them.

Why only these three vessels?

The Kli Yakar points out that all three of these vessels differ in their measurements.

The Aron is two and one-half cubits in length, one and one-half in width, and one and one-half in height.

The Mizbayah is one cubit in length, one in width, and two in height.

The Shulhan is two cubits in length, one in width, and one and one-half in height.

Note that none of the Aron's measurements are whole numbers. The Aron is where the tablets that Moshe brought down from Mount Sinai are kept. Inside the Aron lies the spiritual heritage of the Jewish people. We all know that when it comes to things of the spirit, we can never feel complete. There is always room for improvement and there is always need for improvement. That's why the measurements of the Aron are not whole. It represents the insatiable spiritual need in each of us.

On the other hand, the Mizbayah's measurements are all whole numbers. The Mizbayah was used to bring people closer to God, through sacrifice. The Mizbayah also brought forgiveness for the sinner and made him or her whole again. That's why it is measured in whole numbers — because it makes the Jewish people whole.

The Shulhan's measurements are a mixture of whole and non-whole numbers. It represents the physical nature of this world. Its length and width measurements are whole numbers, implying that in the physical world, we should perceive ourselves as having everything. The world was created for each of us, and we have the right — the obligation — to partake in its wonders.

However, the Shulhan's height wasn't a whole number. This teaches us that we shouldn't overreach. We should never feel whole and complete as far as our personal struggle with our desires is concerned. We should learn to curb ourselves and, like our patriarch Yaacov, feel that we are blessed with what we have. We should, in effect, limit the need to fulfill our egos.

These three items were crowned with gold to represent the crowns that we must wear proudly — the crown of spirituality, the crown of worldly enjoyment, and the crown of humility — throughout our lives.

Only then will our Mishkan, the sanctuary we have inside of us, be filled with the spirit of God.

THE HAFTARAH CONNECTION

(Kings I 5:26)

Our Parsha describes the Mishkan and everything that goes into it. B'nai Yisrael volunteer and contribute whatever they can to participate in this great event.

Our Haftarah describes the building of the First Temple. Now that the Jews have established themselves in the land, they need a permanent structure for God to reside in. The Temple was built by King Solomon, who spared no expense to make it a glorious house for God.

GEMMATRIA God tells Moshe that everyone should bring a *Terumah*, a contribution for the Mishkan. Each person brought as much as he could, eager to donate to God's sanctuary. God says that B'nai Yisrael should bring this contribution *lee*, "to Me." The numeric value of lee is 40.

Much later, when B'nai Yisrael are asked to give a Terumah to the Kohen, the question is asked, How much should a person bring?

The answer is that if someone gives 1 out of 40 bushels to the Kohen, it is considered a generous amount. This amount is derived from the Terumah the Jewish people brought to God's sanctuary to fulfill the command of "lee."

❖

God showed Moshe a vision of what the Mishkan and its vessels were supposed to look like. The Hebrew word *mareh*, "show," is used. Its numeric value is 246.

The Sages say that God sent the angel Gavriel to show Moshe what the Mishkan was supposed to look like. His name has the same numeric value of 246.

TELL IT WITH A SMILE The Rabbi met one of his wealthiest congregants in town. "Philip, I'm so glad to see you," said the Rabbi. "I know you are the major contributor to our Building Fund, and I appreciate that. But tell me, why don't you ever attend synagogue services?"

"Rabbi," Philip answered, "I look to the synagogue for my spiritual health, as I look to the local hospital for my physical health. I contribute to the hospital so that it will be well-equipped in case of an emergency.

"But I hope I never have to go there either!"

תצוה

THIS WEEK IN THE PARSHA

Oil for the Menorah

God tells Moshe that B'nai Yisrael are to bring pure oil to light the Menorah. Aaron and his sons will light the Menorah, which must be kept continually burning.

Clothes of the Kohanim

The clothes of the Kohanim are to be made from gold, sky-blue thread, dark red thread, crimson wool, and linen. Not all the garments worn by the Kohanim need all five types of material.

The ordinary Kohen is to wear four different articles of clothing:

The *K'tonet,* a tunic knitted from linen. Its length depends on the height of the Kohen. It is to reach from his neck to his heels.

The *Mihnasayim,* shorts, are to be made out of linen. They stretch from the waist of the Kohen to his thigh.

The *Mitznefet,* a linen hat.

The *Avnet,* a sash made of linen, is wrapped around the waist of the Kohen.

The Kohen Gadol is the leader of all the Kohanim. He will wear eight garments every day. Four are the same as those of every other Kohen, although the material used to make his clothes might differ. The four additional garments that the Kohen Gadol will wear are:

The *Ephod,* which resembles an apron, is made out of all five materials listed above. It covers the Kohen Gadol's back and front. There are two shoulder straps; each strap has a stone on which the names of six tribes are engraved.

The *Hoshen* is a breastplate, and is also made out of all five materials. It is one cubit in length and half a cubit in width, folded in half to make a square. On the breastplate are four rows of mounted stones; each row has three stones. The name of one of the twelve tribes is written on each stone. Attached to the Hoshen is the *Urim V'tumim*.

The Hoshen is attached to the Ephod with a gold chain and placed over the Kohen Gadol's heart.

The *M'eal*, worn over the K'tonet, is a robe made from sky-blue wool. It has armholes but no sleeves, and a hole for the head. It covers the Kohen Gadol from head to toe, and is worn over the K'tonet.

At the bottom of the M'eal are alternating gold bells and gold pomegranates.

The *Tzitz* is a gold plate engraved with the words, "Holy to God." It is tied across the forehead of the Kohen Gadol.

Moshe Is to Install the Kohanim

God tells Moshe that he is to install Aaron and his sons as Kohanim. Aaron is to immerse in a *mikveh*, and then Moshe will dress him in the special clothes of the Kohanim, and anoint him with oil. God then enumerates the sacrifices that Aaron is to bring at the time of his consecration.

The installation of the Kohanim is to take seven days.

Sacrifices on the Altar

God explains to Moshe which sacrifices will be brought on the Mizbayah. The Kohanim will have to bring a sheep each morning and a sheep each afternoon. This is to be done daily, for all generations.

The Incense Altar

God tells Moshe to build a *Mizbayah Hak'toret*, an Altar for burning incense. Aaron is to burn incense on it every morning and evening. It is to be made of wood, and covered with gold. Its dimensions are one cubit in length, one cubit in width, and two cubits in height.

WISDOM OF THE SAGES

"The sound (of the bells) shall be heard when he enters the sanctuary." (28:35)

Rav Chaim of Brisk couldn't tolerate people shouting out their prayers. He felt that praying should be conducted in a more dignified way. He brought proof of this from the above verse.

Why is it that there are little bells on the M'eal? The bells were put on the M'eal of the Kohen Gadol so that Aaron would be heard when he entered the sanctuary. He could just as easily have prayed out loud and everyone would have known he was coming, but we see that God wanted a more dignified way to indicate the time for prayer.

"Take its (the sacrifice's) blood and put it on Aaron's right ear lobe, right thumb, and right big toe." (29:20)

The ear, thumb, and toe have special significance to the Kohen, the spiritual leader of the people.

The Kohen must evince a willingness to listen to everyone's

problem. He must have open hands to give whatever is needed to his people. He must have swift feet to enable him to do the sacrificial work in the sanctuary and, at the same time, administer to all those who need him.

1. Why did it take seven days to inaugurate the sanctuary, as well as Aaron and his sons? Couldn't this have been done in one day?

2. One of Aaron's jobs was to light the Menorah at night. In the morning, he cleaned it out and made it ready again. Why was this cleaning considered a separate job? Couldn't Aaron have cleaned the Menorah and made it ready a few minutes before lighting, as we do on Hanukkah?

3. The last verse in the Parsha (30:10) deals with Aaron's job on Yom Kippur. Why bring this in now, when the subject matter is the Mishkan?

THE HAFTARAH CONNECTION

(Yehezkel 43:10)

In our Parsha Moshe is told to perform certain rituals in order to purify both the Kohanim and the Mizbayah. These rituals took seven days.

In the Haftarah, Yehezkel receives an image of what the Temple will look like. He is to transmit this image to B'nai Yisrael. At the same time, the prophet is given a ritual that must be performed for seven days. Its purpose is also to consecrate the Kohanim and the Mizbayah.

TABLE TALK
DVAR TORAH

In our Parsha, God tells Moshe that Aaron is to be put in charge of lighting the Menorah. Then Moshe is told to separate Aaron from the rest of the nation. This separation signified the establishment of the priestly tribe. The Kohanim were going to be in charge of everything that went on in the Mishkan.

The sequence of events, however, seems to be backwards. First, God should have declared that Aaron was going to be the Kohen Gadol, and only then should he have given him the job of lighting the Menorah. Why does the commandment to light the Menorah come before Aaron is appointed as Kohen Gadol?

Rabbi Moshe Feinstein explains that the job of lighting the Menorah had nothing to do with Aaron's appointment as Kohen Gadol. The light of the Menorah is symbolic of the light of the Torah. Just as the Menorah had to be lit until the flame could sustain itself, so too a teacher or parent has to kindle the love of learning Torah in a child until he can fan these flames himself.

Furthermore, the oil had to be pure and clear so that it would stay lit for a long time. Likewise, a teacher or parent must explain things to a child in a clear way so that the knowledge will stay with him forever.

Finally, the lamps of the Menorah always had to be filled to capacity, regardless of whether it was a long winter night or a short summer night. So too, teachers have to put in 100 percent of their capacity no matter how intelligent the students may be. It does not make a difference if the child is of average intelligence, super bright, or has a learning problem. The teacher's job is to be like the Menorah, a light for the child.

This helps us understand why Aaron was given the duties of

lighting the Menorah before he was officially appointed the Kohen Gadol. It was to show us that Aaron did not need a position of greatness to be a leader of the people. As a teacher of the people, Aaron was already fit to light the Menorah and bring light to the Mishkan.

GEMMATRIA

God told Moshe to command Aaron to light the Menorah in the Mishkan. The Hebrew word *Tetzaveh*, which means "command," has a numeric value of 501. The words *nashim tzivah*, "He commanded women," also have a value of 501. This teaches us that the lighting of candles is a commandment that women should perform.

TELL IT WITH A SMILE

The people of Benjeen were worried. Rumor had it that there would be no oil to light their Hanukkah menorahs this year. So they gathered at Mendel the Tinker's home.

"Mendel, you have always been good at getting hard-to-find items," declared Berel, the town's spokesman. "But we need a miracle now. We have heard that there will be no oil available for our menorahs this year. You must find us some."

"Of course," Mendel said, eager to help. "I will find you the purest oil for Hanukkah. But don't expect a miracle." And he set out to find oil.

On the night of Hanukkah the townspeople gathered at Mendel's house again.

"Were you able to find oil?" Berel asked.

"Of course!" Mendel exclaimed. He took out a little jar of oil.

"But this is hardly enough for one menorah, let alone for the entire town," cried Berel.

Mendel shrugged, "What, were you expecting a miracle?"

Counting B'nai Yisrael

God tells Moshe that there is a specific way to count the Jewish people. Moshe is to take a half-shekel from every Jewish male over 20 years of age, and then count the money to find out the number of people. Counting B'nai Yisrael in any other way will bring a plague upon the people. The half-shekel is to be used for the upkeep of the Mishkan.

The Washbasin

God tells Moshe to build a *Keyor,* a copper washbasin, with a copper base. It is to be used by Aaron and his sons before entering the *Ohel Moed,* the Tent of Meeting, or when approaching the Mizbayah. Failure to wash their hands and feet will bring punishment by God.

The Anointing Oil

God instructs Moshe how to make the *Shemen Hamishha,* the anointing oil. The formula is never to be duplicated by an outsider or used by anyone except a Kohen. The punishment for using this oil is *karet*, divine punishment.

Betzalel the Architect

God tells Moshe to appoint Betzalel as chief architect of the Mishkan. God has filled Betzalel with great wisdom and understanding. Oholiav will be his assistant.

The Sabbath Day

B'nai Yisrael are told to keep the Shabbat as a sign between them and God. They are to work for six days but rest on the seventh, just as God rested on the seventh day of creation.

The Golden Calf

On Mount Sinai, Moshe receives two stone tablets written with the finger of God.

Meanwhile, the people waiting at the foot of the mountain don't know why Moshe has not come down. They ask Aaron to create an idol to lead them.

Aaron tells them to bring the gold jewelry of their wives and children. He throws the jewelry into a mold from which comes a golden calf. Next, Aaron builds an altar and declares that the following day will be a festival to God.

The people get up early the next morning to sacrifice burnt offerings to the idol.

God tells Moshe to return to the people for they have become corrupt. God says they are a stiff-necked people and that He is ready to kill them and make of Moshe's descendants a great nation.

Moshe hears this and pleads with God not to do such a thing because the Egyptians will say that God took the people out only to kill them in the desert. Moshe also reminds God of the promise He made to the patriarchs to bring the people to the land of Israel. God accedes to Moshe's pleas.

Punishment for Sin

Moshe begins to descend the mountain. When he sees the rejoicing over the golden calf, Moshe gets angry and throws the tablets down, shattering them. He enters the camp, melts down the calf, grinds it into fine powder, and makes B'nai Yisrael drink it.

Aaron tells Moshe not to be angry with the people. He must realize that they have bad tendencies. Aaron then recounts what happened. Moshe realizes that the people are hard to control and that Aaron failed to control them.

Moshe declares that all those who are for God should join him. The tribe of Levi steps forward. Moshe then orders them to kill anyone who committed idolatry, and the Levites kill nearly 3,000 people.

The next day, Moshe goes up the mountain to plead with God to forgive the people for their sin. He tells God to blot him out of the Torah, if God cannot forgive them.

God tells Moshe that He will erase those who sinned against Him. Then God brings a plague upon the nation for what they have done.

God Sends an Angel to Lead the People

As a result of their sin, God will not lead the Jewish people into the land of Israel. They are a stiff-necked people and He might destroy them. Instead, He will send an angel to lead them into the land. When B'nai Yisrael hear this, they mourn.

Moshe is told by God to take the Ohel Moed, the tent in which he speaks to God, and set it up outside of the camp. God will speak to Moshe there face-to-face, just like a person would speak to a friend.

Moshe Sees God's Presence

Moshe asks God to show him His grandeur. God tells Moshe that no one can see Him and live. But God puts Moshe into the cleft of a rock and shows him a vision.

Moshe Receives the Second Tablets

God tells Moshe to carve out two tablets just like the first ones. Moshe then climbs Mount Sinai again.

God gives Moshe additional instructions concerning the people. Upon entering the land, they are to destroy all idols. They may not make a treaty with the people who dwell in the land, so that there will be no intermarriage. They must observe Pesah, and remember that every firstborn belongs to God. They are to observe Shabbat and Shavuot. Three times a year, on Pesah, Shavuot, and Sukkot, every male must present himself to God in Jerusalem. The first fruit of the land has to be brought to the Temple and eaten there.

They are forbidden to eat a young goat cooked in its mother's milk.

When Moshe descends the mountain, his face glows. B'nai Yisrael are afraid to approach him, so Moshe puts a veil over his face. When he speaks to God, Moshe removes the veil, and when he finishes speaking, he replaces it again.

WISDOM OF THE SAGES

"Everyone included in the census must give a half-shekel." (30:13)

Moshe asked everyone to give a half-shekel in order to count the people. Why half a shekel? Wouldn't it have been easier if each of them gave a whole shekel?

There is a saying, "No man is an island." Perhaps we are being told here that no one can achieve perfection by themselves. In order to become whole, you need someone else. No one knew whose half-shekel combined with his own to make a complete shekel. The half-shekel of even the simplest Jew could have united with the half-shekel of the most important Jew to make them both whole.

How could the Jewish people commit the crime of the golden calf?

The Midrash explains that the Jews truly believed in God. Moshe told them that he was going up the mountain and would return in 40 days. The Jews counted the day he went up as the first day, but that was only part of a day. It didn't count. After 40 days, the people didn't know why Moshe hadn't returned. The Satan appeared and told them that Moshe had died. He showed them a picture of Moshe in the sky, dead. The Jews, now leaderless, wanted an intermediary to talk to God, so they asked Aaron to create the calf.

Michelangelo created a sculpture of Moshe with horns on his head. How could he have made such a mistake?

When Moshe descended from the mountain, the Torah says that his face glowed. The Hebrew word for "glow" is *karan*. The same root word in Hebrew also means "horn." Michelangelo read an incorrect translation of the Torah and because of this many people think Jews have horns!

 In the census, everyone from the age of 20 had to give a half-shekel. Why was the age of 20 chosen?

A person could bring the half-shekel only if he was held accountable for his sins. The numeric value of *shanah vamaalah,* which means "(20) years and up," is 506.

The Yerushalmi Talmud points out that a person can only be punished for his sins after the age of 20. This is hinted to in the numeric value of *li'onashim,* which means "for punishment." Its numeric value is also 506.

So, the age of 20 was chosen as the earliest age to bring the half-shekel because it is the earliest age a person is accountable for his sins.

THE HAFTARAH CONNECTION

(Kings I 18:1)

In our Parsha, B'nai Yisrael commit the first really grave sin. Since Moshe was up on the mountain longer than they had thought he would be, they created a golden calf to worship.

During the reign of King Ahab, B'nai Yisrael served Ba'al, a false god. The prophet Eliyahu confronts them and proves that there is only one true God.

Our Haftarah took place 600 years after the sin of the golden calf, but B'nai Yisrael still had not learned their lesson.

While Moshe was on the mountain, B'nai Yisrael sinned by making the golden calf.

Upon seeing them sin, God told Moshe, "Descend, for your nation has sinned." God is so angry that He says to Moshe, "Leave Me alone so that I may destroy them and make you into a great nation."

Moshe raises some legitimate issues in the nation's defense. He claims that the merit of the forefathers of the Jewish people should be enough to prevent God's wrath. He also brings up the anticipated reaction of the surrounding nations: They would claim that God took the Jews out of Egypt just to destroy them.

But Moshe does not refuse, at this point, God's offer to create from him a great nation, in place of the Jewish people. Moshe refutes this point only later on, after he punishes the nation for worshiping the calf. Then he tells God to destroy him, if God won't forgive the nation for their sins. Why didn't Moshe speak up immediately, when God made His proposal?

The Midrash tells us that, indeed, Moshe did reply right away to God. What he said was that if a stool with three legs (Avraham, Yitzhak, and Yaacov) can't stand on its own, then a one-legged stool — founded upon Moshe — doesn't stand a chance of remaining upright.

But that was not enough of a reason for God to let the people survive. So Moshe punished the nation severely, and the nation accepted the punishment without complaint. Now Moshe had something concrete to show God, evidence that the nation regretted their sin, and deserved another chance. If God wasn't willing to accept their repentance, then Moshe told God to erase him from the Torah, since he was their teacher, and was just as much to blame.

Moshe was displaying the traits of a good teacher. When students fail, a teacher must never blame the students alone. He must first realize that the blame rests with him, and find a way to rectify the situation.

1. God tells Moshe that Betzalel will be in charge of building the Mishkan. Right afterwards, the Torah inserts the obligation of keeping Shabbat. What is the connection between the Mishkan and Shabbat?

2. God tells Moshe that He will send an angel to lead B'nai Yisrael into the land, instead of leading them Himself. Moshe immediately complains to God. Compare this with Moshe's reaction (or lack of reaction) to God's words in the Parsha of Mishpatim (23:20-23). Why does he react differently now? What has happened to affect their relationship?

3. The Torah says that God remembers the sins of the fathers for four generations. How can God punish someone for the sin of his great-grandfather?

In this week's Parsha, B'nai Yisrael realized that there is no reward for sin.

When a school survey showed that there was almost no crime among Jewish pupils, the chief of police asked one of the students in the local day school why that was.

"Easy," answered the student. "Crime doesn't pay!"

ויקהל

THIS WEEK IN THE PARSHA

Moshe Instructs B'nai Yisrael

Moshe gathers B'nai Yisrael and tells them not to work on Shabbat. He also tells them that they are not allowed to light any fires on Shabbat.

Then Moshe tells the people about the materials they will need to build the Mishkan. B'nai Yisrael make donations and the skilled workers, men and women alike, volunteer to do the labor.

Moshe lets B'nai Yisrael know that God has designated Betzalel as head architect, and Oholiav as his assistant.

B'nai Yisrael donate so much gold, silver, and other material that Moshe has to ask them to stop. B'nai Yisrael then build the necessary vessels for the Mishkan.

WISDOM OF THE SAGES

This Parsha seems to be a repetition of Parsha Terumah. The Torah could have just said, "And they built all that they were commanded to." Why repeat everything?

When cooking or working, many people try to be creative, adding their own personal touch to what they are doing. A recipe may call for exact measurements, but a creative cook will add a pinch of this or a touch of that in the hope of creating a culinary masterpiece.

But when it comes to instructions from God, exactness

counts. God has already created the masterpiece, you just have to follow instructions. By telling us that B'nai Yisrael did exactly what God told them to do in the building of the Mishkan, we see that the people understood that the instructions from God would lead to the perfect House of God.

"And Moshe assembled the entire community of Israel." (35:1)

Before commanding them to begin building the Mishkan, Moshe assembled the nation. He wanted to be sure the people understood that they had to be united in order to ensure the continuous existence of the Mishkan.

Sure enough, one of the reasons given for the destruction of the Second Temple is disunity of the Jewish people.

"Each person who was ready to volunteer, then came forward." (35:21)

Why doesn't the Torah simply tell us that the volunteers came forward? If they volunteered, then certainly they were ready.

People with good intentions don't always have the opportunity to carry out their good deed, especially regarding finances. They become lazy, letting the opportunity to do what they planned slip away. But when it came to the donations for the Mishkan, everyone who had the intention of contributing actually did so.

TABLE TALK
DVAR TORAH

The K'ruvim were very special, even in comparison to the other vessels. There were two reasons for this. First, they were placed right on top of the Aron in the Kodesh Hakodashim, the Holy of Holies. Second, they were one of the few items that had to be made from one mold of gold. This was no easy task. So, wouldn't it have been much easier to make the K'ruvim in separate parts and then attach the pieces to each other?

Perhaps we can learn something here about reaching our goals in life. We should not do things in fits and starts, especially when it comes to Torah learning. We must not wait to learn when we find time, learning one day, skipping the next day, then maybe learning a bit the day after. This kind of patchwork learning lacks continuity, and we end up with many seams in our Torah knowledge. Rather, we should set goals for ourselves, set times for learning, so that we can maintain a regular pattern of learning Torah.

Another explanation of why the K'ruvim were made of one mold lies in our understanding what they represent.

The Sages say that one K'ruv represents God, and the other K'ruv represents B'nai Yisrael.

These two K'ruvim, molded from one piece of gold, show the strength of the connection between God and B'nai Yisrael. We know that anything made out of one mold is much stronger than something glued together. It has no seams that might cause it to crack under pressure.

The K'ruvim were set upon the Aron, where the Torah was kept. This represents the fact that God and B'nai Yisrael are an unbreakable mold built upon a base of Torah. Just as the Aron served as the base for the K'ruvim, so too must the Torah serve as the base of our connection with God. When that is done, our tie with God will be of one mold, pure and unbending.

1. Usually, the east is considered a direction of great importance. The sun rises in the east, signifying a new day. Why then was the Mishkan built facing west?

2. In describing the attributes of those who participated in the building of the Mishkan, the Torah calls them *haham lev,* "wise of heart." Isn't that a contradiction? Wisdom is in the brain, while emotions are in the heart.

3. The washbasin of the Kohanim, the Keyor, was made of something very unique — mirrors that the women donated. Why?

THE HAFTARAH CONNECTION

(Kings I 7:40)

In Parsha Terumah, Moshe received instructions on how to build a sanctuary for God. Our Parsha relates the actual building of that sanctuary.

Our Haftarah deals with the actual building of the Temple that King Solomon erected for God.

TELL IT WITH A  The Rabbi of a very large congregation passed away and went up to heaven. At the gates, the angel in charge looked over the Rabbi's merits and faults and gave him the keys to a Cadillac, as befit his status. The Rabbi went out for a spin, in order to see what status his former friends had achieved. He saw some with slightly better cars, but the bulk of those he saw drove standard Fords.

Suddenly, a big six-door limousine went by. It had every convenience imaginable. The Rabbi honked his horn and the driver pulled down his tinted window. The Rabbi was shocked at what he saw. There, sitting with a cigar in his mouth, was Chaim, the synagogue bus driver.

The Rabbi quickly turned his car around and drove back to the angel.

"How could this be?" sputtered the Rabbi. "The bus driver of my synagogue drives a limousine and I, the Rabbi, have a Cadillac?"

"Chaim has many more merits than you," explained the angel. "When you got up to give a sermon, you used to put people to sleep. But the way Chaim drove the bus, people never stopped praying!"

GEMMATRIA   *Vaya'as Betzalel et ha'Aron*, "And Betzalel made the Aron" (37:1)

The name *Betzalel* has the numeric value of 153. This is the same value as the words, *B'tzel El*, "In the shadow of God."

God gave Betzalel certain wisdom. One example of this wisdom is that only Betzalel knew how to make the Aron. It was a secret process that only someone who walked in the "shadow of God" was permitted to know.

פְּקוּדֵי

THIS WEEK IN THE PARSHA

The Completion of the Mishkan

All the donations for the Mishkan are counted, and then used as required. The garments for the Kohanim are sewn. B'nai Yisrael complete the Mishkan and bring it to Moshe for inspection. Moshe is pleased with the results, and blesses the workers.

Moshe erects the Mishkan on the first day of the first month, in the second year after the Exodus from Egypt.

He puts all the vessels in their proper places.

In the middle of the Kodesh Hakodashim is the Aron. On top of the Aron are the K'ruvim.

The Menorah is in the southern part of the Mishkan. The Shulhan is in the northern part, opposite the Menorah. The Mizbayah Hak'toret is in the middle.

In the Courtyard, the Mizbayah is placed on the eastern side, 10 cubits from the entrance.

The Keyor is placed between the entrance to the Mishkan and the Mizbayah, toward the southern part of the Courtyard.

A Cloud Covers the Mishkan

A cloud descends over the Mishkan, filling the Ohel Moed with God's glory. With the cloud there, Moshe is unable to enter.

When the cloud lifts, it is a sign that B'nai Yisrael have to travel. God's cloud remains on the Mishkan by day, and fire is on it at night, so that the Mishkan is always visible to B'nai Yisrael as they travel.

WISDOM OF THE SAGES

Hazak Hazak Ve'nithazayk!

This Parsha completes the reading of the Book of Shemot. When we finish reading one of the five books of the Torah on Shabbat, we say *hazak hazak ve'nithazayk!*

"Be strong, be strong, and we will grow stronger."

The word hazak is really a combination of the three words — *harisha,* "plowing"; *zreah,* "planting"*; ktzirah,* "harvesting."

Before planting a field you must plow the ground to make the earth soft and ready. Then you plant a seed and nurture it until it has grown. Unless you go into the field daily and tend to the seeds, they will not reach maturity. Ultimately, if you have done your job, you will harvest your field.

So too, a person who begins to study Torah must first lay the groundwork; he must prepare his mind and open it to the possibilities that the Torah has to offer. He must nurture what he has learned by reviewing it time and time again. Only then will he reap the fruits of his labor.

That is why we say, "Be strong, be strong, and we will grow stronger," at the end of each book of the Torah. A Jew must gather his strength whenever he finishes learning a part of the Torah; then he must begin again, reviewing what he has learned. In this way, he solidifies his knowledge, he adds to the knowledge of the community, and we all become stronger.

"These are the accounts of the Mishkan." (38:21)

Moshe showed us that when collecting money from others — whether large or small sums — an exact accounting has to be given. It doesn't make a difference how honest or reliable you are, or others consider you to be. When it comes to other people's money, there can be no room for doubt.

"There were a total of 100 bases for the boards of the Mishkan, made out of 100 talents." (38:27)

The 100 boards of the Mishkan had 100 bases. Our Sages say that everyone should say 100 blessings a day. Just like the bases keep the sanctuary standing, the blessings we say each day are the foundation of our relationship with God. By blessing God, we show that belief in God is the base upon which we build our lives.

Isadore went up to his local Rabbi and said: "Rabbi, can you please make me a Kohen?"

"No, I can't make you a Kohen," replied the Rabbi. "It's just not in my powers."

"Please," implored Isadore, "it's very important for me to be a Kohen. I'll even give a donation of 500 dollars to the synagogue."

But the Rabbi insisted that his hands were tied.

Isadore wouldn't take no for an answer. "Listen," he told the Rabbi, "I'll give you a check and you can fill in any amount you want, just please make me a Kohen."

The Rabbi's curiosity was greatly aroused. "Isadore," the Rabbi explained, "you have to understand, it's not a matter of money. But tell me, why do you want to become a Kohen so badly?"

"Well, you see," replied Isadore, "my father was a Kohen and his father before him was a Kohen, so I too want to be a Kohen!"

TABLE TALK DVAR TORAH

After B'nai Yisrael finished making the different parts of the Mishkan, they brought all the sections to Moshe.

The Midrash explains, however, that after the sections were put together, the Mishkan couldn't be lifted by the people because the beams were too heavy.

The Midrash adds that they brought it in sections so that Moshe could erect it. Since he hadn't taken part in the actual work of the Mishkan, God wanted him to do this. The Midrash points out that when Moshe saw that the people could not lift the beams, he himself complained to God. How was he expected to get the Mishkan standing if the whole nation couldn't do it? God told him to place his hands beneath the beams. When he did this, the beams miraculously rose, making it seem as if Moshe himself raised the Mishkan.

Rabbi Rudman explains that the Midrash teaches us something about *avodat Hashem*, serving God. In any spiritual activity, the outcome isn't the only important thing. The effort that you make to achieve the goal is important as well.

Eyov (Job) 5:7 says that "Man is born to toil." When people have nothing but time on their hands, they are joyous at first but, after a while, they become distraught and upset. They don't know what to do with themselves. The reason for this is that man was born with an innate desire to work and feel productive. This explains why the Sages tell us, "Praiseworthy is he who toils in Torah." Since a person has a desire to toil and work, he should direct his efforts toward excelling in Torah.

But when they feel the work is too hard, people tend to give up. They suppress their need to be productive if they think the obstacles are too great. That's how many wonderful projects are abandoned.

In our Parsha, B'nai Yisrael — and Moshe — felt that putting the Mishkan together was too great a job. They were ready to give up, without expending supreme effort.

That is why God told Moshe to place his hands under the beam. God was telling Moshe and the people that even an impossible task can be done, if only you try. As Jews, we believe that with God's help, the impossible can be accomplished. As a nation, we are living proof of that.

So Moshe put his hands under the beams and, miraculously, they rose. When he made the effort, God helped him to accomplish his task.

 The numeric value of Mishkan is 410. This corresponds to the number of years that the First Temple stood in Jerusalem, before being destroyed.

THE HAFTARAH CONNECTION

(Kings I 7:51)

In our Parsha, the building of God's sanctuary is completed. The walls are erected and all the vessels are put in their proper places.

After the sanctuary is complete, God makes it his resting place. A cloud descends on it.

Our Haftarah also deals with the completion of the Temple that King Solomon built.

Here, too, a cloud descended on the Temple, signifying that God had made this his resting place.

1. Moshe blessed the people when they brought the finished parts of the Mishkan to him. Why didn't he wait and bless them after the Mishkan was standing?

2. Why were the vessels put in their specific places? What does this tell us about the different vessels?

ABOUT THE
HOLIDAYS

WISDOM
OF THE
SAGES

Rabbinic pearls of wisdom.

 FOR YOUR INFORMATION

Outlines basic laws of the Holiday.

 TABLE TALK
DVAR TORAH

A brief, cogent talk that can be repeated at the Holiday table.

 The Torah Reading

A simple, straightforward explanation of the Holiday reading.

Hanukkah occurs every year on the 25th day of the Jewish month *Kislev*.

There are two miracles that we celebrate on Hanukkah:

(1) *Rabim b'yad me'atim* – "Many given over to the few"

More than 2,000 years ago the Greek king, Antiohus, decreed that the Jewish people would no longer be allowed to keep three commandments:

Shabbat: The foundation of the Jewish belief in the creation of the world by God.

Hodesh: The power of the Jewish court in Jerusalem to declare the new moon and thus control when the Jewish holidays fall out.

Brit Milah: The symbol of the covenant between God and the Jewish people.

Antiohus knew that these three commandments were basic to the existence of Judaism. Without them, Greek culture would soon overpower the Jewish nation as it had so many other nations.

Eventually, the Greek king went so far as to force Jews to bow down to the Greek idols. Some Jews bowed down, while others gave their lives to sanctify God's name.

In the town of Modiin there lived a family of Kohanim led by Matityahu the Maccabee. When he saw a Jew bowing to one of the Greek idols, he killed him. Before the Greek soldiers could kill Matityahu, he fled to the mountains. There, together with his five sons, he started a revolution against the Greeks. Many Jews joined the revolution.

Though greatly outnumbered, and armed with very few weapons, the Maccabees succeeded in defeating the greatest army of that time. This miraculous victory was seen as a clear manifestation of God's love for the Jewish people.

(2) Nes pah hashemen – "The miracle of the jug of oil"

After the great victory, the Jews went back to the Temple in Jerusalem. They wanted to resume the daily service, which the Greeks had stopped. Part of the service included the lighting of the Menorah. However, all the pure oil needed to light the Menorah had been defiled by the Greeks.

Ultimately, one small, sealed jug of pure olive oil was found. There was enough oil in the jug to last for exactly one day. A miracle occurred, and the oil lasted for eight days — enough time to make new oil. That is why the Jewish people celebrate Hanukkah for eight days.

WISDOM
OF THE
SAGES

Why is this holiday called Hanukkah?

Hanukkah is a combination of two words: *Hanu,* "they rested," and *kah*, which has a numeric value of 25. Together these words indicate that the Jews rested on the 25th day of the month of Kislev, which is when Hanukkah begins.

Another meaning for Hanukkah is "dedication." Since the Greeks had profaned the Altar, the Maccabees rededicated it.

TABLE TALK
DVAR TORAH

The Bait Yosef asks a famous question about Hanukkah:

Why do we celebrate Hanukkah for eight days? There was enough oil to last for one day, so the miracle lasted seven days, not eight.

While the Sages present more than 100 answers to this question, here are a few of the most famous:

It is true that the miracle of the oil lasted only seven days, but we celebrate Hanukkah for another reason as well. The rededication of the Altar and vessels also warranted a celebration, and it took eight days to rededicate them.

We can also divide the celebration of Hanukkah into two parts. The first day was a celebration in commemoration of the victory of the Jewish people over the Greeks. The other seven days were a celebration of the miracle of the oil.

Another commentator suggests that since they knew it would take eight days to make new oil, the Maccabees only put one-eighth of the oil in the Menorah. In this way the Menorah would be lit for at least a short time. A miracle occurred, and the little bit of oil lasted all night. When they put another eighth in the next night, it too lasted all night and so on for all eight nights.

Finally, one of the most interesting answers to the Bait Yosef's question lies in the significance of numbers to the Jewish people. The number eight indicates God's covenant with the Jewish people. That is why the brit milah is done on the eighth day.

The Jews saw in their victory a renewal of their covenant with God. He gave them not only a physical victory, but also helped them to achieve a spiritual victory against the most amoral nation in the world, the Greeks. So it was fitting that the Jewish people celebrate their victory for eight days.

FOR YOUR INFORMATION

1) To publicize the miracle of Hanukkah we light the candles of the menorah at a window at night, when people are coming home from work.

2) The candle for each night must burn for at least half an hour.

3) Put the candles into the menorah from right to left, but light the candles from left to right.

4) On the first night say three blessings before lighting the candles:

Baruh atta....l'hadlik ner shel Hanukkah.

Baruh atta....she'assa nisim la'votaynu ba'yamim ha'haim ba'zman ha'zeh.

Baruh atta.....she'heheyanu v'keyemanu v'hegeyanu la'zman ha'zeh.

On the other seven nights, the third blessing is omitted.

5) During the day, we say the Hallel, "Praise to God," prayer.

6) It is customary to eat potato pancakes (latkes) or jelly doughnuts *(sufganiyot)* since they are fried in oil, and oil is such a major ingredient in this holiday.

7) Parents give children Hanukkah *gelt* (Hanukkah money) or presents.

8) The *dreidel,* a special spinning top, has four Hebrew letters — *nun, gimel, hey, shin* — which are the first letters of *nes gadol hayah shahm,* "a great miracle occurred there" (in Israel).

The dreidel game has a number of variations. It starts by everyone putting a candy into the middle. One person spins the dreidel. If it lands on gimel, the person takes everything. If it lands on hey, the person takes half. If it lands on nun, the person gets nothing. If it lands on shin, the person has to put in another candy.

The Torah Reading

The daily Torah reading during Hanukkah is from Bamidbar 7:1-8:4.

This section of the Torah deals with the dedication of the Altar. It lists the different gifts that the heads of the twelve tribes brought. On Hanukkah, we also celebrate the fact that the Jews dedicated the Altar and the different vessels.

The reading also deals with the commandment to light the Menorah in the Mishkan. On Hanukkah, we too light a menorah.

Purim occurs on the 14th day of the Jewish month of *Adar.*

(In some places in Israel it occurs on the 15th day of Adar.)

The story of Purim is detailed in *Megilat Esther,* the Scroll of Esther, which is read during the holiday.

Megilat Esther tells the story of how King Ahashverosh of Persia marries Esther, a Jewish woman, just as Haman, the king's evil advisor, prepares to destroy the Jewish people. Mordechai, Queen Esther's relative, tells her that she must do everything in her power to save the Jewish people. At great risk to herself, Esther enters the king's chambers and invites him to a party. At the party, she announces that Haman is planning to kill her people. The king orders Haman killed on the day he chose to kill the Jews. Then the king permits the Jews to take arms against those who would destroy them.

The Jews fought on the 13th of Adar and rested on the 14th. The people of Shushan, the capital of Persia, fought on the 13th and 14th, and rested on the 15th. The days they rested from battle were declared days of rejoicing for all future generations. People gave gifts to one another, and distributed charity to the poor.

WISDOM
OF THE
SAGES

Why is this holiday called Purim?

In Hebrew, the word *purim* means "lottery." This refers to the lottery that Haman held to select the day to kill the Jews.

TABLE TALK
DVAR TORAH

When Mordechai learned of Haman's decree — that all the Jews were to be killed — he immediately tore his clothes as a sign of mourning. But when Esther heard the news, she sent him new clothes so that he would stop mourning.

Why did Esther relate to the news of Haman's decree so differently than Mordechai? She must have understood the gravity of the situation. Wouldn't it have been more effective if she, too, had changed out of her royal robes and into clothes of mourning?

The Tiferet Shlomo says that Esther wanted to prove a point. Mordechai tore his clothes because he thought the way to convince God that the Jewish people were worthy of redemption was to show contrition.

Esther, on the other hand, felt that God would never let His people be destroyed. Rather than mourn and succumb, a Jew must be happy and secure in the belief that God will save him. That's why she sent Mordechai new clothes, to show him that he should not give up, that God is waiting in the wings to save His people.

That also explains why there is no mention of God in the Megilah. God could have brought plagues to Persia as He had to Egypt, but instead, He chose to remain in the background. God wanted to see if the people would believe in Him strongly enough to continue with their lives in the face of adversity and know that, once they had done all they could, God would step in.

Sure enough, soon after Esther sends Mordechai new clothes, we see that he is dressed in the king's clothes and led through the city by none other than Haman. It is from this point in the Megilah that things start looking up for the Jews.

FOR YOUR INFORMATION

1) We are obligated to hear the Megilah reading twice on Purim — once at night and once in the morning.

2) The Megilah must be read from a parchment scroll.

3) Before we begin reading, we recite three blessings:

Baruh atta....al mikrah Megilah.

Baruh atta....she'assa nisim la'votaynu ba'yamim ha'haim ba'zman ha'zeh.

Baruh atta.....she'heheyanu v'keyemanu v'hegeyanu la'zman ha'zeh.

4) When reading the Megilah, it is customary to twirl a *grogger*, "noisemaker," to drown out the name of Haman.

5) There are three additional commandments on Purim: to give *shalah manot*, portions of food to our friends and neighbors; to give *matanot la'evyonim*, presents to the poor; and to eat a *seudat Purim*, a festive Purim meal.

6) It is customary to dress up on Purim as a symbol of the hidden things that go on in the Megilah.

 # The Torah Reading

During the day, in addition to reading the Megilah, we also read from Shemot 17:8-16, which deals with the victory of B'nai Yisrael over Amalek. Amalek was the first nation to enter into battle with the Jews after they left Egypt. Although the Jewish people won, God promised to erase all remembrance of Amalek, because they alone dared attack the Jews even after hearing the miracles God had done for them. The Purim story is another example of Amalek, in the guise of Haman, trying to destroy the Jews. Once again, the Jewish people are triumphant.

Sources: Wisdom of The Sages

B'raishit

Lech Lecha: "The whole land" — Panim Yafot

Vayera: "Sarah told Avraham" — Rashi

Toldot: "And Yitzhak loved" — Imray Hen

Vayetzay: "I will serve" — Midrash Rabbah
"And in the morning" — Tractate Megilah (13b)

Vayislah: "Save me" — Beit HaLevi
"And Yaacov asked" — Rabbi Y"L Hesman
"And Esav said" — Hafetz Haim

Vayeshev: "And the pit was empty" — Oznayim Latorah
"In three more days" — Rabbi Shapira of Lublin

Meketz: "And the second child" — Imray Yitzhak

Vayegash: "And Yosef told" — Z. Hillel
"And behold your eyes" — Ahavat Yonatan
"And Yaacov said" — Baalay Hatosafot

Vayehi: "Zevulun will live by the seas" — Hafetz Haim

Shemot

Shemot: "Take your shoes" — Olilot Efraim

Vaera: "And these are the heads" — Rabbi M. Ben Yair

                          "And I will harden" — Rabbi Shmuel Wintraub

Bo: "The Jews had light" — Rabbi Yisrael of Rizhin

                          "These words" — Nefesh Yehuda

B'shalah: "God will fight" — Rabbi Yonatan Iveshitz

                          "And B'nai Yisrael called it mahn" — Kli Yakar

                          "As long as Moshe" — Mishnah Rosh Hashanah 3:8

Yitro: "So you shall" — Raayonot Hadrush

                          "And they stood" — Hafetz Hayim

Mishpatim: "He shall cure him" — Maayanah Shel Torah

Terumah: "Speak to B'nai Yisrael" — Parparot Latorah

                          "Cover it with pure gold" — Tzvi Yisrael

Tetzaveh: "Take its blood" — Hahmay Yisrael

Ke Tesah: "Everyone included in the census" — Hahmay Yisrael

Vayakhail: "And Moshe assembled" — Hahmay Yisrael

"Each person" — Rav Chi"da

Pekuday: "There were a total of 100 bases" — Hidushay Har"im

MY
D'VAR
TORAH
FOR...

MY D'VAR TORAH FOR...

MY D'VAR TORAH FOR...

MY
D'VAR TORAH FOR...

MY
D'VAR TORAH FOR...

MY D'VAR TORAH FOR...

MY
D'VAR TORAH FOR...

MY
D'VAR TORAH FOR...